NEW YORK

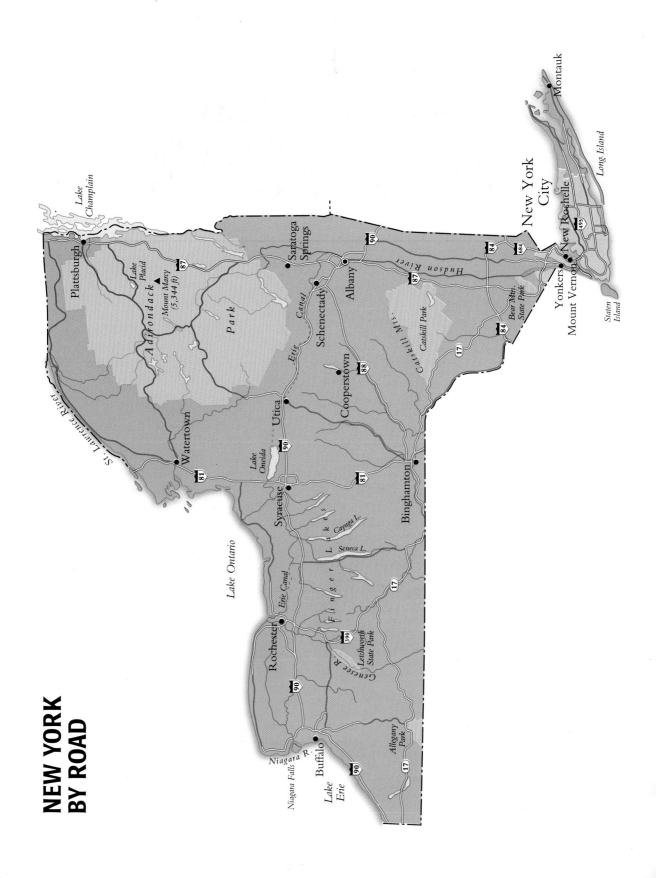

NEW YORK
BY ROAD

Lake Champlain

Plattsburgh

Adirondack

Lake Placid

Mount Marcy
(5,344 ft)

Park

87

St. Lawrence River

Watertown

81

Saratoga Springs

Erie Canal

Schenectady

90

Albany

87

Hudson River

84

684

New York City

Yonkers

New Rochelle

Mount Vernon

495

Long Island

Montauk

Staten Island

Bear Mtn.
State Park

84

Catskill Mts.

Catskill Park

17

Cooperstown

88

Utica

90

Lake Oneida

Binghamton

81

Lake Ontario

Syracuse

Erie Canal

Finger Lakes

Cayuga L.

Seneca L.

17

Rochester

390

Letchworth
State Park

Genesee R.

90

Allegany
Park

Niagara R.

Buffalo

90

17

Niagara Falls

Lake Erie

CELEBRATE THE STATES
NEW YORK

Virginia Schomp

Benchmark Books

MARSHALL CAVENDISH
NEW YORK

To Chip,

who makes being a mom

the best job in any state

Benchmark Books
Marshall Cavendish Corporation
99 White Plains Road
Tarrytown, New York 10591-9001

Copyright © 1997 by Marshall Cavendish Corporation

Printed in Italy

Library of Congress Cataloging-in-Publication Data
Schomp, Virginia.
New York / by Virginia Schomp.
p. cm. — (Celebrate the states)
Includes index.
Summary: Surveys the geography, history, economy, people, and state highlights of New York.
ISBN 0-7614-0108-3 (lib. bdg.)
1. New York (State)—Juvenile literature. [1. New York (State)] I. Title. II. Series.
F119.3.S36   1997   917.47—dc20   96-1878   CIP   AC

Maps and graphics supplied by Oxford Cartographers, Oxford, England

"The New Colossus" music copyright © 1992 by Jerry Silverman

Photo research by Ellen Barrett Dudley

Cover photo: *Photo Researchers, Inc.*, Andy Levin

The photographs in this book are used by permission and through the courtesy of: *Photo Researchers, Inc.*:
Alan L. Detrick, 6-7; B. Yarvin, 10-11; George Haling, 13, 117; Jeff Lepore, 19; Allen Green, 22; Margot
Granitsas, 46-47; Freer, 56; Bill Backman, 61; Bonnie Rauch, 63; Richard Hutchings, 65; George Ranalli, 66;
David M. Grossman, 68-69; Grantpix, 71; David M. Grossman, 73; Ellan Young, 77; Peter Miller, 81; Katrina
Thomas, 83; Ray Ellis, 84; Michael P. Gadomski, 102-103; Jerry Cooke, 108 (bottom); Joseph Sohm, 112;
Larry Mulvehill, 113; Catherine Ursibol, 119; Wesley Bocxe, 120; Gregory K. Scott, 123 (top); Bonnie Sue,
125; Nancy D'Antonio, 137; Richard Hutchings, back cover. *New York State Department of Economic
Developement:* 14, 64, 111. AP/Wide World Photos: 16, 52, 78, 79. Peter Arnold: Fred Bavendam, 20, 123 (bottom). *Steve Stanne/Hudson River Sloop/Clearwater Inc.:* 25. *New York State Historical Association, Cooperstown:*
26-27, 33. *Collection of the New York Historical Society:* 31, 40. *Corbis-Bettmann:* 36, 41, 43, 92, 99, 133, 135
(bottom). *UPI/Corbis-Bettmann:* 50, 93, 97, 130 (left), 131 (top). *RonChar Photo Art/Ronald Thomas,
Photographer/Charlene Scanlon, Hand Colorist:* 54. *The Image Bank:* Mel Digiacomo, 58, Marvin E. Newman,
72, 88- 89; Jules Zalon, 74; Frank Whitney, 138. Photofest: 95, 96. *Reuters/Corbis-Bettmann:* 101, 129, 130
(right), 131 (bottom), 135 (right). *Courtesy of the Adirondack Museum:* 108 (top). *James Marshall, Brooklyn
Image Group/The Fund:* 116. *Springer/Corbis-Bettmann:* 132. *Mark Kurtz Photography:* 136.

3   5   6   4

CONTENTS

NEW YORK IS...

New York is people . . .

"Here individuals of all nations are melted into a new race of men."
—French settler St. Jean de Crèvecoeur

"I am the Mayor of a city that has more Jews than live in Jerusalem, more Italians than live in Rome, more Irish than live in Dublin, more blacks than live in Nairobi and more Puerto Ricans than live in San Juan."   —former New York City mayor Ed Koch

. . . and unforgettable places.

"I find in . . . New York . . . the best and most effective medicine my soul has yet partaken—the grandest physical habitat and surroundings of land and water the globe affords."
—poet Walt Whitman

"A bulger of a place it is. The number of the ships beat me all hollow."   —frontiersman Davy Crockett, visiting New York City

No state has a richer history.

"The land of Ganono-o or 'Empire State' as you love to call it, was once laced by our trails from Albany to Buffalo . . . trails worn so deep by the feet of the Iroquois that they became your own roads of travel."   —a Cayuga chief

"To Europe she was America, to America she was the gateway of the earth. But to tell the story of New York would be to write a social history of the world."   —writer H. G. Wells

No state is so loved . . .

"I'm a regular visitor to the Adirondacks. My sons and I go camping, fishing, and hunting. Let me tell you, there's no better place on earth for roasting the perfect marshmallow and discussing who caught the biggest fish."   —Jim Bigness, Schenectady

"I came from the Dominican Republic. The water there is dirty sometimes. In New York, the lakes and rivers are so clean and beautiful. There's lots of woods to play in. I like the color of the leaves in fall."   —Dayana Gomez, fifth grader, Monticello

. . . and so unappreciated.

"I don't like the life here. There is no greenery. It would make a stone sick."
—former Soviet premier Nikita Khruschev, visiting New York City

---

Most of all, New York is contrasts. It is mighty factories and towering cities. It is quiet villages, rolling farmland, unspoiled wilderness. New York is millions of people from a variety of cultures all laughing and arguing in a noisy symphony of voices. There's no other place like it. With all its contrasting treasures, New York is a state bursting with life and full of surprises.

1 GATEWAY TO AMERICA

In ancient times, New York was one vast plain, with a line of high mountains in the north. Colossal glaciers ground their way across this dull land. They rounded the mountaintops, carved lakes and valleys, and dumped dirt. By the time the ice melted, New York had been transformed, with a new landscape that was varied and spectacular.

"MAGICAL SHAPES"

New York's landscape includes four different types of landforms: upland, plateau, lowland, and coastal plain.

Upland. In the east of the state are two mountainous regions, the Adirondack Upland and the New England Upland. The Adirondack Upland is a circle of hills and mountains, including Mount Marcy, New York's highest peak, at 5,344 feet. Thickly forested, the Adirondacks are wild and beautiful, with hundreds of lakes, streams, and waterfalls. The New England Upland includes the wooded Taconic Mountains and the low hills of Manhattan Island, heart of New York City.

Plateau. Perched like a high table above surrounding lowlands, the Appalachian Plateau, in southern New York, is the state's largest land region. Here storybook character Rip Van Winkle slept among the "magical hues and shapes" of the Catskill Mountains.

The Tug Hill Plateau sits at the center of the state. Centuries ago, this flat, rocky region was connected to the Appalachians.

Lowland. New York's low plains hold the state's most fertile farmland. The narrow Saint Lawrence Lowland runs along the Saint Lawrence River to Canada and then east to Lake Champlain. The Great Lakes Lowland, which touches Lakes Erie and Ontario, is dotted with swamps and rounded hills called drumlins. Within

Jet black soil from ancient lake bottoms makes the lowland village of Florida a perfect place for onion farming.

Long Island's sandy beaches offer a great escape from New York City on hot summer days.

the Hudson-Mohawk Lowland are the green valleys carved out by the Hudson and Mohawk Rivers.

Coastal Plain. The low Atlantic Coastal Plain takes in Long Island and three boroughs (sections) of New York City—Queens, Brooklyn, and Staten Island. Long Island stretches 120 miles from the lower edge of Manhattan. Its southern shore is fringed with sandy ocean beaches.

A WEALTH OF WATERS

From Lake Tear-of-the-Clouds on high Mount Marcy, the Hudson River begins its journey three hundred miles south to the Atlantic Ocean. Near its mouth, this majestic river rises and falls with the ocean tides. Native Americans called it "the water which flows two ways."

Another major New York river is the Saint Lawrence. This waterway on the New York-Canadian border flows out of Lake Ontario. A scattering of rocky islands, called the Thousand Islands, dots the blue waters where lake and river meet.

Farther west, the short but powerful Niagara River thunders down a rock ledge at Niagara Falls. French missionary Father Louis Hennepin was the first to write in awe of the "incredible Cataract or Waterfall, which has no equal."

New York's waters also include nearly eight thousand lakes. Many of these nestle among the hills and mountains of the Adirondacks. Two of the Great Lakes, Erie and Ontario, share their shores with both New York and Canada. Lake Champlain sits on New York's border with Vermont. Oneida Lake, in central New York, is the largest lake completely inside the state. To its west are the eleven Finger Lakes, long narrow strips of deep blue scooped out by the ancient glaciers.

CLIMATE CONTRASTS

Summer temperatures in New York City can climb to 95°F and above. High humidity makes it feel even hotter. "Working in the city in the summer—forget about it," says printing-press operator Kerry Marie. "The streets are like . . . a steambath. If I didn't work in air-conditioning, I wouldn't survive." Summer is cooler inland and in the mountains. In the central Adirondacks, July averages a pleasant 66°F.

Winter brings even greater contrasts. By the ocean, in Manhattan and Long Island, winter temperatures hover around the freezing mark, 32°F. It isn't much colder beside Lakes Erie and Ontario, but winter squalls can dump an incredible amount of snow. Great Lakes cities such as Rochester, Buffalo, and Syracuse are often buried under one winter storm after another.

After a winter storm blanketed New York City in January 1996, airports and businesses struggled to reopen, while schoolchildren enjoyed an unexpected holiday.

The coldest parts of New York are the Saint Lawrence Valley and the upland and plateau regions. Winters there are long, and temperatures often drop below zero. Tug Hill Plateau, blanketed with 225 inches of snow a year, is the snow capital of the east.

New Yorkers take even the coldest, snowiest winters in stride. In fact, they often turn them into a celebration. Cities and towns by the Great Lakes and in the Appalachians and Adirondacks salute snow season with winter carnivals. The fun includes snow sculpting, dogsled races, and sports such as broom hockey, snow softball, and volleyball on ice. Saranac Lake, in the northern Adirondacks, is the frosty setting for America's oldest winter festival. Activities center around a sparkling ice palace built from more than fifteen hundred huge blocks of ice cut from nearby Lake Flower.

WILD THINGS

New York's great variety of land features and weather makes it a perfect home for many different plants and animals. More than half of the state is covered with forests. There are about 150 types of trees, both evergreens and hardwoods. Many types of wildflowers bloom, including the black-eyed Susan, violet, wild rose, and the humble dandelion.

Peek under a wildflower and you may see the animal that outnumbers all others in New York—the mouse. In remote mountain areas live the black bear and wildcat. Graceful white-tailed deer roam the forests. New York's countryside is home to shy rabbits, woodchucks, porcupines, and black-masked raccoons. Even city parks offer a cozy spot for chipmunks and bushy-tailed squirrels.

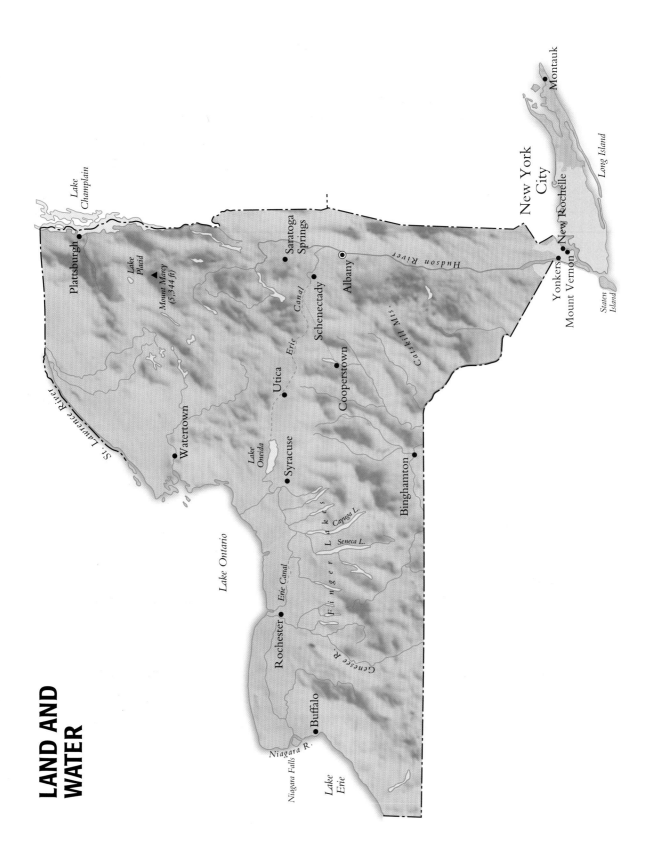

LAND AND WATER

Montauk

Long Island

New York City

New Rochelle

Yonkers

Mount Vernon

Staten Island

Lake Champlain

Plattsburgh

Saratoga Springs

Albany

Hudson River

Lake Placid

Mount Marcy (5,344 ft)

Erie Canal

Schenectady

Catskill Mts.

Cooperstown

Utica

Watertown

Lake Oneida

Syracuse

Cayuga L.

Seneca L.

Binghamton

Finger Lakes

St. Lawrence River

Lake Ontario

Erie Canal

Genesee R.

Rochester

Buffalo

Niagara R.

Niagara Falls

Lake Erie

Small in size but big in numbers, the white-footed mouse.

New York's three hundred types of birds include both seasonal visitors and year-round residents. Summer brings blackbirds, red-breast robins, and the clatter of woodpeckers rapping on tree trunks. A familiar signal of autumn are the honking calls from V-shaped flocks of Canada geese heading for winter homes in New York. Best-known of the state's year-round bird residents is the fierce-looking bald eagle.

Many birds take their meals in New York's lakes and rivers. These freshwaters are home to silvery trout, salmon, and spiny-finned sunfish. Bays and coastal waters teem with saltwater fish, including flat-bodied flounder, which change color to match the sea bottom. For the fisherman—feathered or human—who is willing to pry open a hard shell, Long Island's shores offer plenty of fat clams and oysters.

A BIRD BOUNCES BACK

If you're ever walking along New York's shoreline and a tiny gray bird dive-bombs your head, don't get mad—get out of there. Chances are your attacker is the least tern, and your big feet are demolishing its bedroom.

Thirty years ago, this dainty eight-inch seabird seemed headed for extinction. First, hunters shot thousands of them for their feathers. Laws were passed protecting the least tern from hunting. Then growing crowds of New York beachgoers began to invade tern nesting grounds.

The least tern lays two small eggs in a shallow scrape of ocean sand. Splashes of brown and lavender make the eggs blend into the beach. That helps protect them from hungry raccoons, rats, and gulls, but not from careless people. "On many occasions," says conservationist Joel Cook, "I've watched people . . . walk through a least tern nesting site, crushing eggs and chicks underfoot."

Concerned New Yorkers today are working to prevent this kind of destruction. Groups such as Long Island's Huntington Audubon Society and Hempstead Conservation Department have posted signs around least tern nesting grounds. Local volunteers help make sure people keep out. The least tern is still an endangered species, but conservationists are hopeful that these protection efforts will restore the silvery gray flocks to New York's shorelines.

PEOPLE PLACES

Until the 1960s, New York had more people than any other state. Today California and Texas are bigger, but New York is still BIG. Its estimated population in 1994 was 18.2 million. A whopping 7.3 million, or 40 percent of all those people, live in New York City.

Geography explains those numbers. New York City sits on one of the largest and best natural harbors in the world. Many ships anchor in the deep harbor waters, surrounded almost completely by land that protects them from ocean storms. The broad Hudson River forms a passageway leading far inland from New York Harbor. Since the days of the first white settlers, this meeting of ocean and river has made New York City a magnet for business and a gateway for outsiders entering America. "There is no city in the world that has a greater influence," wrote historian Thomas Adams. "Outside America, New York is America."

Geography, along with weather, also helps explain the way people have settled other parts of New York. Where would you build your house—where the land is flat and fertile and the weather's mild, or on thin, rocky soil in the cold mountains? Probably, if you settled outside New York City, you'd join most other New Yorkers in the fertile lowlands that run along the Hudson and Mohawk Rivers and west to the Great Lakes. Large cities dotting these regions include Buffalo, Rochester, Syracuse, and the state capital, Albany.

Fewer people live in southern New York, on the rugged Appalachian Plateau. Binghamton is this region's only large city. Sprinkled among the hills and forests—especially around the Finger Lakes and in Catskill Mountain valleys—are smaller cities

A cargo ship unloads at a Brooklyn pier. New York City's fine harbor has made it one of the leading ports of the world.

and towns. Farms and orchards also hug the banks of the Saint Lawrence River and Lake Champlain in the north.

Least populated of all are New York's far northern tip and the Adirondack Mountains. Long, frozen winters and stony soil in these regions have discouraged all but the hardiest New Yorkers.

MAKING A MESS

"The landscape still overwhelms the people." That's how writer Edmund Wilson summed up New Yorkers' endless struggle to tame their beautiful, rugged environment. Eighty-five percent of all New Yorkers crowd around a few large cities, and the rest gather mostly in small towns and villages. Around these pockets of people stretch mile after mile of forests, fields, lakes, and mountain wilderness.

Not that people haven't made their mark on the state. Ever since the first Dutch settler's shack rose beside the Hudson, New Yorkers have been building. Their busy hands have produced homes, offices, factories, highways, canals, bridges, and more. Sadly, wherever people build, environmental problems are sure to follow.

New York's air, water, and ground have been badly polluted. City dwellers breathe unhealthy fumes from cars, trucks, power plants, and factories. Rain washes some of the pollution out of the air to fall as acid rain, damaging forests and poisoning lakes and streams. Wastes pumped out by businesses and city sewers further foul New York's rivers. "Hudson is the worst," says Doug Herrmann, a police officer with New York City's scuba-diving patrol. "One time we were diving there, I came up with toilet paper . . . all over me."

Garbage is another environmental mess. New Yorkers toss out more than 18 million tons of trash a year, and the state is running out of places to put it. Most garbage is buried in smelly landfills. Rotting wastes can leak from old, unlined landfills, polluting water supplies underground.

Pollution and destruction of habitat (an animal's natural environment) have endangered many of New York's native creatures. The once-common timber wolf, mountain lion, cougar, otter, and mink have disappeared from the state. Nearly eighty other types of animals are growing scarce. Along the shores, endangered animals include the largest living sea turtle, the leatherback, and the humpback whale, famous for its high leaps and haunting songs. The fast-flying peregrine falcon and the majestic bald eagle are also in danger of disappearing forever.

CLEANING IT UP

New York's environmental problems are big. Fortunately, so are its plans for solving them. In fact, the state has one of the best environmental protection and conservation programs in the country.

Over the past twenty years, pollution controls have cleaned up the air and water. Populations of some endangered fish and animals are increasing. People are recycling more of their garbage. Millions of acres of forests and other environmentally important lands have been bought for protection by the state government. The state is also cleaning up polluted lands and turning some of them into parks. In 1995, a 113-acre landfill in Croton-on-Hudson, near Manhattan, became the beautiful green Croton Point Park. While standing on a hill of wildflowers topping sixty years of buried trash, New York environmentalist John Cronin said, "We're dancing on the grave of a giant."

The progress is encouraging, but there's still much work to be done. Thick layers of pollutants still line the bottoms of many waterways. Hundreds of toxic-waste sites around the state wait for cleanup. It will take many years and millions of dollars to correct all the mistakes of the past. But New York is facing its mistakes with serious solutions that promise a cleaner, healthier future.

CELEBRATING THE HUDSON

About thirty years ago, New York folksinger Pete Seeger and some friends came up with an idea for teaching people about Hudson River pollution. They decided to build a traveling environmental school. To raise money for the project, they held an afternoon of music . . . and came up with just $167.

Today the *Clearwater* sails the Hudson River. This copy of the great wooden sailing ships that once filled the river stops in town after town, teaching people how to keep the Hudson clean. That first afternoon concert has grown into one of the country's biggest and best music festivals, Clearwater's Great Hudson River Revival. For two days each June, at Valhalla, in the Hudson Valley, a variety of musical sounds flow nonstop from six different stages. Stilt walkers, jugglers, and mimes stroll among the crowds, and booths offer foods from many different cultures. And, of course, there are exhibits calling attention to the Hudson's problems and how New Yorkers can be a part of solving them.

2 THE PATH TO EMPIRE

A scene from James Fenimore Cooper's book The Last of the Mohicans

Four hundred years ago, five Native American nations battled for the land that would become New York State. A warrior named Hiawatha grew sick of the bloodshed. He called a meeting of the warring chiefs. The five nations—Mohawk, Oneida, Onondaga, Cayuga, and Seneca—agreed to unite under a Great Tree of Peace. Their union became known as the Iroquois League, the most powerful force in north America.

THE MIGHTY IROQUOIS

Tribes from Canada south to Virginia and as far west as Illinois learned to fear the Iroquois war cry. Even the Algonquians, New York's oldest Native American group, were forced to surrender ancient lands. But fierce warriors were only part of the secret behind the Iroquois' power.

Each Iroquois nation elected leaders called sachems to attend a governing council. At council meetings, the sachems talked over problems and disagreements. Their decisions helped keep their confederacy united and strong.

Only men could be sachems. Iroquois men were also warriors and hunters. Armed with stone clubs and bows and arrows, they searched the forests for deer, moose, bear, and other meat. Women

HOW BEAR LOST HIS TAIL: AN IROQUOIS STORY

In the old days, Bear had a long black tail. He liked to wave it about, for everyone to admire. That old trickster Fox saw this, and laughed. He decided to play a trick on Bear.

It was wintertime, when Hatho, the Spirit of Frost, covers the lakes with ice. Fox made a hole in the ice. He surrounded the hole with fish. Just as Bear walked by, Fox dipped his tail in the water and pulled out a juicy trout.

"Would you like to try?" Fox asked.

"Oh, yes," said Bear.

"Then come, Brother, we will find you a good spot."

Fox knew that fish stay in deep waters when Hatho covers their lakes. He made a hole in the ice where the water was shallow. He told Bear to place his tail in the water. He said, "Do not look and do not move. When a fish grabs your tail, I will shout."

Fox sneaked home and went to bed. In the morning, he returned. He laughed when he saw a small black hill, covered with snow, snoring. Quietly, he crept near. "Bear! Now!" he shouted.

Bear woke with a start. He pulled his tail with all his strength. But the lake had frozen over, and his tail broke off—snap! Bear turned to see the beautiful fish he had caught. Instead, he saw his long black tail, caught in the ice.

So it is that today Bear has a short tail and no love for Fox. Sometimes you may even hear a bear moaning when he thinks of his beautiful lost tail.

planted and harvested corn, beans, and squash. From the forests they gathered wild nuts and berries. In some ways, Iroquois women were more powerful than the men. They owned all the land and property, and decided which sachems spoke in council.

Council meetings took place around the fire in an Iroquois longhouse. These large barn-shaped buildings of log and bark were home to twenty or more families. Each family had its own small compartment, with bark-lined beds and storage shelves. On winter days, parents and children liked to gather around the fire in the long center aisle to hear an elder tell the ancient stories of their people.

THE EUROPEAN "INVASION"

"We found a very pleasant place, situated amongst certain little steep hills, and there ran down into the sea a great river." That's how Italian explorer Giovanni da Verrazano, the first white person ever to see New York, described his "discovery" in 1524 of its sparkling harbor. After a quick look, Verrazano headed back to sea. Later visitors from Europe would stay longer, changing life in the region forever.

Samuel de Champlain, a French explorer, hiked south from Canada in 1609. Beside the large lake later named Lake Champlain, he claimed the north's woods and waters for France. That same year, Henry Hudson, an Englishman working for the Dutch, sailed his ship, the *Half Moon,* through New York's harbor and up a majestic river. Hudson was searching for a shortcut through North America to Asia. He was disappointed when he came to the river's end. Still, he brought back news of friendly natives willing to trade furs for guns and whiskey.

By the mid-1600s, Dutch trading posts lined "Hudson's river." The most important were Fort Orange and New Amsterdam. Fort Orange was a small, rough village 150 miles upriver. Muddy New Amsterdam sat at the mouth of the Hudson, on the island Native Americans called Man-a-hat-ta—"land of hills."

Most Native Americans (the Europeans called them "Indians") welcomed the Dutch. They were glad to trade furs for the settlers' guns, blankets, liquor, and other goods. As the newcomers took

An early view of New Amsterdam, in 1679. A visitor to the small settlement remarked that it was only " . . . the commencement of a town to be built there."

over more and more land, there were some native attacks on settlements. Mostly, though, the Indian nations fought among themselves for control of fur trade routes and hunting grounds.

The Europeans battled, too, over their end of the fur trade. In 1664, England anchored four warships in New Amsterdam harbor. Dutch governor Peter Stuyvesant—known as Peg Leg Pete for his wooden leg—stomped and stormed but surrendered without a shot. Fort Orange was renamed Albany, in honor of England's Duke of York and Albany. The village of New Amsterdam and the new British colony itself were named New York.

Soon after, England and France went to war over control of North America. Many of their battles were fought in New York. Algonquians supported the French, but the fierce Iroquois fought for their trading partners, the British. The long, hard-fought French and Indian Wars ended in 1763, with the defeat of France.

DIVIDED AND UNITED

Who were the New Yorkers who cheered British victory in 1763? In many ways, they were just like New Yorkers today—an astonishing mix of different ethnic groups, both divided and strong.

New York colony had always attracted settlers from many lands. There were the Dutch and English. There were people from France, Germany, Ireland, Scotland, Finland, Sweden, and Denmark. New Englanders, called Yankees, moved down from Connecticut and Massachusetts. Black people, some free but mostly slaves, came from the West Indies and Africa.

Many of these people came to New York for its religious

Cidermaking *by W. M. Davis. Dutch governor Peter Stuyvesant planted the state's first apple orchard on his New Amsterdam farm, and early settlers enjoyed dried apples and apple cider.*

tolerance, or acceptance of different faiths. In their homelands, they could not freely practice their religions. New York, like the Dutch government that founded it, welcomed Protestants, Quakers, Catholics, and Jews.

Tolerance didn't mean people always got along. Small farmers quarreled with rich landowners, who owned all the best farmland. By the 1700s, three-quarters of all New Yorkers were farmers, working land they rented from the colony's thirty or so wealthiest families. Other New Yorkers made their living through a trade or handicraft. Merchants bought and sold goods, cobblers made shoes, coopers made barrels. There were bakers, barbers, black-smiths, and more. Many of these businesspeople and many religious groups, too, had their own small political parties, which quarreled over differing interests in meetings of the colony's government.

Still, as much united the colonists as divided them. Nearly every-one lived in a small slice of eastern New York, within a few miles of the Hudson River or New York Harbor. Most people depended on the waterways for transporting goods. All feared the Iroquois, who controlled the western wilderness. In the years following the French and Indian Wars, a new concern united New Yorkers—a growing dissatisfaction with British rule.

REVOLUTION'S BATTLEGROUND

The long wars with France had been costly for the British. To raise money, they came up with new taxes for Americans. That angered New Yorkers, and they led the other colonies in a boycott, in which people refused to buy British goods. The protest was successful. Some of the taxes were canceled. But it was too late. Colonists who were tired of British control were ready to fight for independence.

One-third of the battles of the American Revolution were fought in New York. Britain planned to separate New England from the southern colonies, and New York, smack in the middle, was key to that plan. In 1776, soon after Americans announced their Declaration of Independence, British troops captured New York City, a prize they would hold to the end of the war. Important battles raged in northern New York, including, in 1777, the Battle of Saratoga. France, learning of the colonists' first major victory, at the tiny town of Saratoga, joined the war on the American side.

Not all Americans supported the fight for independence. New York had more British supporters, or Loyalists, than any other colony. Most lived in British-held New York City. The Iroquois, too, were loyal to their old trading partners. When Iroquois warriors under British command attacked New York settlements, General George Washington sent troops to take revenge. The soldiers burned Indian croplands and villages, smashing the Iroquois so completely that their nations would never rise in power again.

In 1783, a thirteen-gun salute thundered over Manhattan. Britain had signed a peace agreement recognizing American independence. Five years later, New York approved the United States Constitution, becoming the new nation's eleventh state.

THE EMPIRE STATE

Northern farms and villages lay in ruins, and one-third of Manhattan had burned to the ground. No state suffered more from the Revolution than New York, and none bounced back so quickly or so high.

With the defeat of the Iroquois, western New York was open to settlers. Yankee farmers piled all they owned in covered wagons and headed for the wilderness. Meanwhile, the sounds of rebuilding rang out across New York City, America's temporary capital until 1790.

Growth halted during the War of 1812. This struggle between

the United States and Great Britain over shipping rights lasted two years, with much fighting along the New York-Canadian border.

When the war ended, the rush for land resumed. Thousands of settlers swept west and north, carving fertile farms from forestland. Highways were built over ancient Indian paths. Robert Fulton's new steamboat paddled the Hudson. But a better way was needed to carry goods between New York's port and its growing frontier.

Many people laughed when Governor De Witt Clinton suggested

Battle of Lake Champlain: McDonough's Victory, *1866. In one of the most decisive battles of the War of 1812, American ships under the command of Captain Thomas McDonough defeated a powerful British fleet on Lake Champlain.*

CELEBRATING HISTORY

Sackets Harbor, New York, was the site of two important battles of the War of 1812. Each July, this charming village on Lake Ontario brings those conflicts alive again, at the Can-Am (Canadian-American) Festival.

Hundreds of people gather around broad green Sackets Harbor Battlefield as the fight begins. Smoke rises and the crowd cheers. The uniformed American "soldiers" are blasting their cannons at the broad-sailed British warships attacking the harbor. The sea battle moves to land, as the soldiers use rifles and bayonets to drive off a wave of red-coated invaders.

Then it's back to the present to celebrate victory. Crowds jam the village's main street for music and dancing. Street-side tents hold tables of barbecued chicken and homemade strawberry shortcake. There are crafts and carnival rides, a parade and fireworks. The party lasts all weekend and is enjoyed by more people than tiny Sackets Harbor sees the rest of the year put together.

building a waterway to connect the Great Lakes and the Atlantic Ocean. How would "Clinton's Ditch" cross more than 360 miles of forests, swamps, and mountains? In 1825, doubters joined the cheering crowds as Clinton led a fleet of flat-bottomed barges down the Erie Canal.

The canal connected Lake Erie, on New York's western border, with Albany, on the Hudson River. Now farmers could ship fruits and vegetables clear across the state and down the Hudson to New York Harbor. Crops and products flowed from western New York and the midwestern states through the canal for shipment overseas.

LOW BRIDGE! EVERYBODY DOWN
(Fifteen Years on the Erie Canal)

Barges carrying passengers and freight through the Erie Canal were towed by mules who strolled along at a leisurely rate.

By Thomas S. Allen

We better be on our way old pal,
Fifteen years on the Erie Canal.
'Cause you bet your life I'd never part
    from Sal,
Fifteen years on the Erie Canal.
Get up there, mule, here comes a lock,
We'll make Rome 'bout six o'clock.
One more trip and back we'll go,
Right back home to Buffalo. *Chorus*

I don't have to call when I want my Sal,
Fifteen years on the Erie Canal;
She trots from her stall like a good old gal.
Fifteen years on the Erie Canal,
I eat my meals with Sal each day,
I eat beef and she eats hay,
She ain't so slow if you want to know,
She put the "Buff" in Buffalo. *Chorus*

A busy Erie Canal town, around 1830. Towns and cities sprang up out of untouched wilderness all along the historic canal.

By 1831, almost one-third of all goods leaving the United States passed through New York State. Over half of all the goods that came into the country also passed through New York.

New York City was the busiest port in the world. Its success attracted new businesses—banks, shipbuilders, newspapers, and more. Towns along the Erie Canal also mushroomed into busy cities. Factories in Buffalo, Rochester, Syracuse, and Utica processed wheat and other products. By 1850, New York had over 3 million people, more than any other state. It was the nation's leader in manufacturing and trade. Many people called New York the crown of the growing American empire.

THE GILDED AGE

In 1843, Isabelle Bomefree heard the voice of God commanding her, "Go East." The freed slave from Ulster County, New York, began touring the country, speaking out for abolition (the ending of slavery) under the name Sojourner Truth.

New Yorkers led the nation in the fight against slavery, illegal in the state since 1827. But not everyone supported abolition. In fact, during the Civil War, which began in 1861, poor workers in New York City rioted. They were enraged by the new draft law that forced them to risk their lives fighting for abolition. Still, New York sent more soldiers to the North's Union army than any other state, and its farms and factories contributed wheat, weapons, and other war supplies.

Sojourner Truth. Abolitionist Frederick Douglass described this freedom fighter as a " . . . strange compound of wit and wisdom, of wild enthusiasm, and flint-like common sense."

The years from the war's end in 1865 to the beginning of the twentieth century were called New York's Gilded Age, when some claimed city streets were paved with gold. New industries multiplied. Factories produced iron, steel, clothing, glassware, magazines, and electrical equipment. New York City's Isaac Singer was one of the inventors of the sewing machine. Rochester prospered, producing George Eastman's new handheld Kodak camera. In Yonkers, Elisha Otis started a company to manufacture his new electric elevator.

This outpouring of products was largely the work of newcomers from foreign shores. In the 1830s and 1840s, immigrants had poured in from Ireland and Germany. After 1880, a new wave arrived, including Italians, Greeks, and Polish and Russian Jews. Attracting all these people was America's promise of religious tolerance and financial opportunity. Millions passed through New York Harbor, the gateway to America, and many stayed to make New York their home. By 1900, one-third of all New Yorkers had been born in another country.

Life wasn't easy for these newcomers. Many worked seven days a week in filthy, unsafe factories. New York City's immigrant neighborhoods were overcrowded slums, with four or five people to a room. British writer Charles Dickens, visiting the Irish neighborhood known as Five Points, declared, "All that is loathsome, drooping, and decayed is here." Still, through hard work, many immigrants climbed from poverty to make good lives for themselves and their families.

From 1914 to 1918, World War I halted the flow of immigrants from Europe. Black families moved from small farms in the

An Italian mother and her children, one family among the millions of
immigrants who passed through New York Harbor in the 1800s.

POPULATION GROWTH: 1790–1990

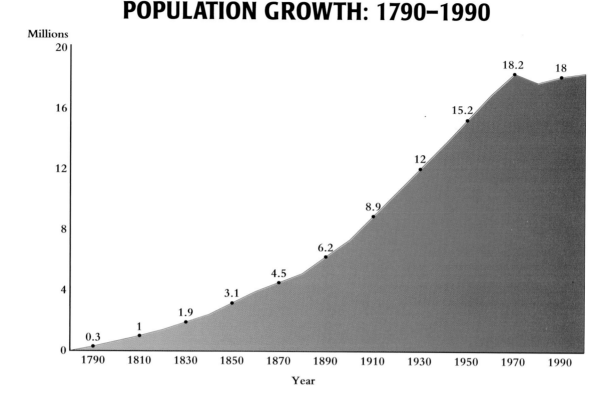

Millions

American South to fill factory jobs. More than five hundred thousand New Yorkers fought in the war. Returning soldiers were welcomed with ticker-tape parades in New York City, the second-largest city in the world.

FACING THE FUTURE

There seemed to be no limit to how big New York City or the state could grow. Then, in the 1930s, the Great Depression taught all Americans their limits. This period of economic hardship began with a crisis at New York City's stock exchange, where stocks—shares in the ownership of U.S. businesses—were bought and sold. In 1929, share prices suddenly fell sharply. Stockholders lost millions of dollars, and many businesses across the country were forced to shut down. One-third of New York's male workers, along with millions of other Americans, couldn't find jobs. President Franklin D. Roosevelt, a native New Yorker, helped Americans through these desperate times. Roosevelt's New Deal programs created jobs and fed the needy.

The Depression ended and America's economy boomed in the 1940s as factories geared up for World War II. New York manufactured an incredible twenty-three billion dollars' worth of planes, ships, and other materials for the troops overseas.

After the war, more southern blacks plus immigrants from Puerto Rico, Cuba, and the West Indies came to New York. They have faced great challenges in their new home. Many businesses, seeking lower taxes and cheaper land, have moved west or south. Cities today battle unemployment, poverty, and crime. In New York City especially, differences among ethnic groups often lead to violence.

But New York is still the Empire State, a world leader in manufacturing and finance. In spite of its serious problems, New York City remains the economic and cultural center of the world. And, as in the earliest colonial days, New Yorkers are still a mix of many peoples, with a history of tackling challenges and coming out strong.

3 HEAD, HEART, AND HANDS

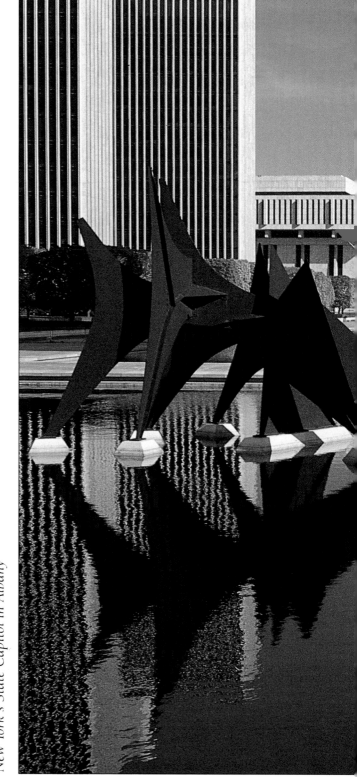

New York's State Capitol in Albany

New York's budget (spending plan) in 1995 was $33 billion—greater than the budget of many countries. Eighteen million New Yorkers, from different regions, ethnic groups, and economic classes, have an interest in how that money is spent. Many of them produce products and services that help pay that gigantic bill. It is government's job to keep the economy strong so that New York will be a good place to produce those goods and services. It is also government's greatest challenge to make sure New Yorkers with differing interests have a fair say in how their state is run.

INSIDE GOVERNMENT

The government of New York is divided into three branches: executive, legislative, and judicial.

Executive The head of the executive branch is the governor, elected to serve four years. New York's governor appoints thousands of judges and government officials, prepares the state budget, and can veto (reject) proposed laws. It's a powerful position, and over the years, New Yorkers have chosen high-powered leaders to fill it.

Four New York governors have become U.S. presidents: Martin Van Buren, Grover Cleveland, Theodore Roosevelt, and Franklin D.

Roosevelt. Van Buren entered law school at age fourteen and won his first case two years later. Cleveland was a hardworking president who often stayed at his desk until two or three in the morning. Theodore Roosevelt became famous during the Spanish-American War when he led his Rough Riders—a gang of cowboys and football players—in a charge up San Juan Hill, Cuba. Franklin Roosevelt was thirty-nine when the disease polio crippled his legs. Seven years later, he ran for governor and won. As president, Roosevelt led Americans through the Great Depression and World War II, assuring them, "The only thing we have to fear is fear itself."

The other top leaders of the executive branch are the lieutenant

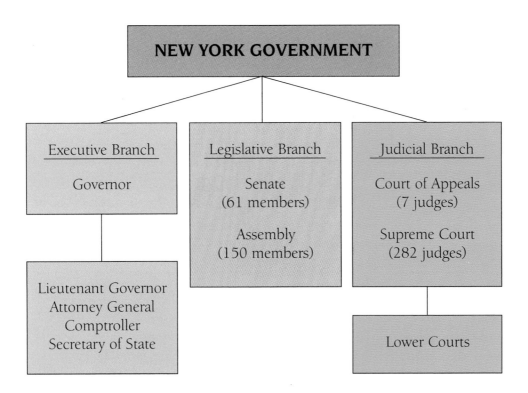

President Franklin D. Roosevelt and First Lady Eleanor Roosevelt, returning to the White House after the president's third inauguration, in 1941. Though he spent many years in Washington, Roosevelt always thought of his Hyde Park, New York, birthplace as home.

governor, attorney general, and comptroller. The lieutenant governor stands ready to serve when the governor cannot. The attorney general is the state's top lawyer. The comptroller manages New York's financial records.

Legislative New York's legislature is divided into two houses: a senate with 61 members and an assembly with 150 members. Each legislator is elected for two years to speak for the people of a particular district, or section of the state.

The legislature's most important job is to create laws. After the senate and assembly agree on a proposed law, called a bill, it goes to the governor. If the governor signs the bill, it becomes a law. If the governor vetoes the bill, it still can become a law, but only if two-thirds of the senate and assembly vote to override (overturn) the veto.

New York's legislature has had its own share of strong leaders. Shirley Chisholm served in the assembly in the 1960s. A tiny woman with a ringing voice, Chisholm pushed through laws to help blacks and Puerto Ricans get a fair chance at a college education. In 1969, Chisholm became the first black woman ever elected to the U.S. Congress. "It's sad, really," she said. "It should have happened years ago."

Judicial New York has a busy and complicated court system. The highest court is the court of appeals, with seven judges. Next come the supreme court, then thousands of lower courts that handle cases in special areas of responsibility or in certain counties, towns, or villages. All these courts make decisions on many matters, from crimes to divorces to complaints against the state.

Some New Yorkers believe their court system is too complicated. They argue that confusion over which courts should handle which cases leads to courtroom delays and jails crowded with people awaiting trial. "This confusing system wastes time and money," says Chief Administrative Judge E. Leo Milonas. Milonas and other judges want to combine some of New York's courts to make "a single, unified court" that could deliver "fair and reasonably swift justice."

Mayors and Managers The government of New York is based in the state capital, Albany. Much of the day-to-day work of government, though, takes place in thousands of small offices across the state.

New York is divided into sixty-two counties, each with its own

Mayor Ed Koch greets Clara Hale, director of Hale House, a New York charitable home for children, in 1988. Being the mayor of New York City, Koch said, "is a tremendous responsibility, but there is no other job in the world that compares with it."

legislature or governing board. Counties are divided into cities, towns, and villages. Each of these, too, has its own local government, run by a mayor, manager, or council.

New York City is a special case. It is divided into five boroughs—Manhattan, Brooklyn, Staten Island, Queens, and the Bronx. All five boroughs are governed by one powerful mayor. The city's mayors have included some of government's most colorful characters.

Jimmy Walker, in the 1920s, was fun-loving, likable . . . and a crook. Walker got to work at three in the afternoon and spent his evenings in nightclubs. While he partied, his gangster friends emptied the city treasury.

In stepped Fiorello La Guardia, smart, honest, and unpredictable. Mayor La Guardia booted out the gangsters and crooked cops. To show he was serious about clobbering crime, he kept an ax handy for chopping up illegal slot machines.

Mayor Ed Koch, in the 1980s, had a habit of speaking his mind. That often got him into trouble with voters, legislators, governors, and even presidents. Koch never apologized. "I have always tried to tell the whole story," he explained, "warts and all."

GOVERNMENT'S "HEART"

"It is our solemn duty," said former New York governor Thomas E. Dewey, "to show that government can have both a head and a heart." New York shows its heart in generous programs that serve its citizens in need. In fact, New York spends more than any other state on public-service programs, including education and social services for the poor.

This photograph of students in a Manhattan elementary school was shown in an exhibit called Midtown West: One School, One World. *"There are sixty different cultures represented in that school," says Charlene Scanlon, who colorized Ronald Thomas's photos. "It's a celebration of different cultures."*

Education is the state's most costly public service. Over two and a half million boys and girls attend New York's 4,068 free public schools. About $9,000 a year goes to educating each student. That's more than is spent by any other state except New Jersey.

A small portion of the money for education comes from the federal government. The rest is paid by the state and hundreds of local school districts. School districts are like small governments running the schools in their area. The state department of education oversees them all.

Every year, there's a huge battle as the governor, legislature, and school districts all argue over how much of the state's budget should go to education and how much of *that* should go to each district. Wealthy districts have more money to spend on schools, so they receive less state aid. Poor districts need and receive more.

The system is supposed to give all children an equal chance at a good education. Many New Yorkers say it doesn't work out that way. New York City, for example, gets a huge slice of state education aid, but it's not enough to meet the needs of the city's nine hundred thousand students. Many young people don't get special services they need, such as English language training. Many schools are so crowded that some classes meet in hallways and storage closets. A recent study found that city school buildings are crumbling, with loose bricks and windows held together by tape. Queens computer teacher Rosemary Weydig had to move seats away from the windows of her third-floor classroom "because the glass is shaking. . . . The panes fall out constantly."

Nearly half of New York City students come from poor families. Many of these families receive help from social service programs. More than 2 million New Yorkers benefit from these programs, which offer medical care, low-cost housing, food stamps (used to buy groceries), and other services to the poor, homeless, elderly, disabled, and others in need.

Rose Pena gets $290 a month from New York's welfare program to care for her two young children. She is using part of her welfare check to pay for a job-training program. Pena wants to get off welfare, she says, because, "You have to earn what you get in life." Joseph Hennesey ran his own business until he lost his legs. New York's health-care program sends a housekeeper to do his laundry and shopping. Without her, he says, "I would lose my apartment and have to go to a nursing home."

The federal government orders states to provide these kinds of services, and it helps pay for them. That still leaves a big bill for state and local governments. In New York, that bill runs into billions of dollars each year.

Recent New York governors have searched for ways to control

Poverty haunts the streets of Manhattan's Spanish Harlem and other inner-city neighborhoods.

those huge costs. Governor George E. Pataki's 1995 budget included deep cuts to social services.

Pataki and his supporters argued that the cuts were needed to help the state's economy. "I understand New York's long-term history and commitment to those less fortunate," said the governor, "and I believe this budget will allow us to continue that." Others disagreed. Hundreds protested outside the State Capitol Building, and Catholic Bishop Howard Hubbard of Albany called Pataki's plan "a much meaner budget than we've seen probably ever in the history of the state."

IT'S THE LAW

New York's government tries to balance a generous heart with a strong arm. A powerful police force—the third largest in the nation—protects New Yorkers and fights crime.

In 1994, New York had the twenty-third highest crime rate of all the states. The crime rate has dropped every year since 1990. In New York City, thanks to tough police work, crime fell 17.5 percent in 1995—the biggest drop in city history. Even criminals are taking notice. One drug dealer complained to a reporter, "I'm telling you the police is out there now, know what I'm saying? And they're serious."

One of the reasons for New York's dropping crime rate is tough gun controls. To buy a pistol in the state, you have to wait about six months while the seller checks to make sure you've never committed a crime. What about criminals who steal or borrow their guns? To catch them, New York City police have started searching

The red-bereted Guardian Angels is a citizens' group that patrols New York City's streets, keeping watch against crime.

suspicious-looking characters stopped for minor lawbreaking, like drinking beer in public. Since the searches began, murders and shootings have dropped sharply. Arturo Garcia, who works in a high-crime neighborhood, explains, "With all the police vigilance [watchfulness], nobody dares carry their guns."

The state is tough on crime in other ways, too. Drunk drivers face fines from $500 to $1,000 and up to a year in prison. Environmental Protection laws include strict punishments for polluters.

Social-service officers handle cases of child abuse. They usually try to help families solve their problems, but if that doesn't work, a safer home is found for the child, and the abusers face punishment in family court.

New Yorkers seem to want a government that's tough on crime. In 1994, when George Pataki ran for governor, he pledged to sign the death penalty into law. Pataki was elected, and in 1995 New York carried out its first execution in thirty-two years.

ECONOMIC POWERHOUSE

Government and business are partners in a strong state. Government programs depend on the taxes and fees paid by businesses and workers. New York has seen some tough times, but it has always survived and grown stronger. That's because hardworking New Yorkers have used their land's riches to make their state a business giant.

The heart of the giant beats in New York City. The city is America's business capital, a leader in many areas, including finance, insurance, shipping, printing, and publishing. Most jobs among the gleaming city skyscrapers and crowded streets are in service industries—companies that provide services instead of products. People who work for banks, advertising agencies, schools, doctors' offices, stores, and restaurants all have service jobs.

Manufacturing used to be New York City's main industry. Many companies still make products, including clothing, scientific instruments, and electrical equipment. But many small, old-style manufacturing jobs are dying out. "Everything is going . . . all the

1992 GROSS STATE PRODUCT: $498 BILLION

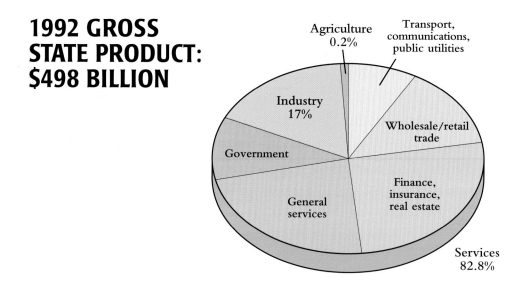

Agriculture 0.2%

Transport, communications, public utilities

Industry 17%

Government

General services

Wholesale/retail trade

Finance, insurance, real estate

Services 82.8%

small industries," says Saul Gever, one of the city's few remaining shoemakers. "Handbags, shoes . . . I feel like the last of a kind."

High-tech jobs are also multiplying to the east of the city, on Long Island. More than nine hundred companies there do scientific research and create space-age medical tools and computer products. Down the road from the modern laboratories, neat rows of cabbages and potatoes grow on hundreds of "truck farms." Vegetables from these small farms are trucked to New York City markets. Joining them on the highways are greenhouse flowers, farm-raised ducks, and barrels of clams and oysters gathered from the salt waters of Long Island Sound.

Agriculture is important along the Hudson River, too. Farmers grow vegetables and fruits, especially apples, and raise chickens for eggs and cows for milk. Service jobs and manufacturing also flourish in the Hudson Valley. Many small cities have grown up around one industry, sometimes around one company. Troy makes shirts. Schenectady, hometown of the General Electric Company, makes electrical equipment. IBM, the giant computer manufacturer, employs thousands of people in offices in Armonk and in nearby labs and manufacturing plants. In Albany, government itself is the main employer.

Western New York's cities also have their specialties. Syracuse makes electrical and electronic equipment. Rochester is the center of the photographic industry. More flour is ground in Buffalo's mills than in any other city in the world.

Just a short drive from Manhattan's skyscrapers are the flowing farmlands of eastern Long Island.

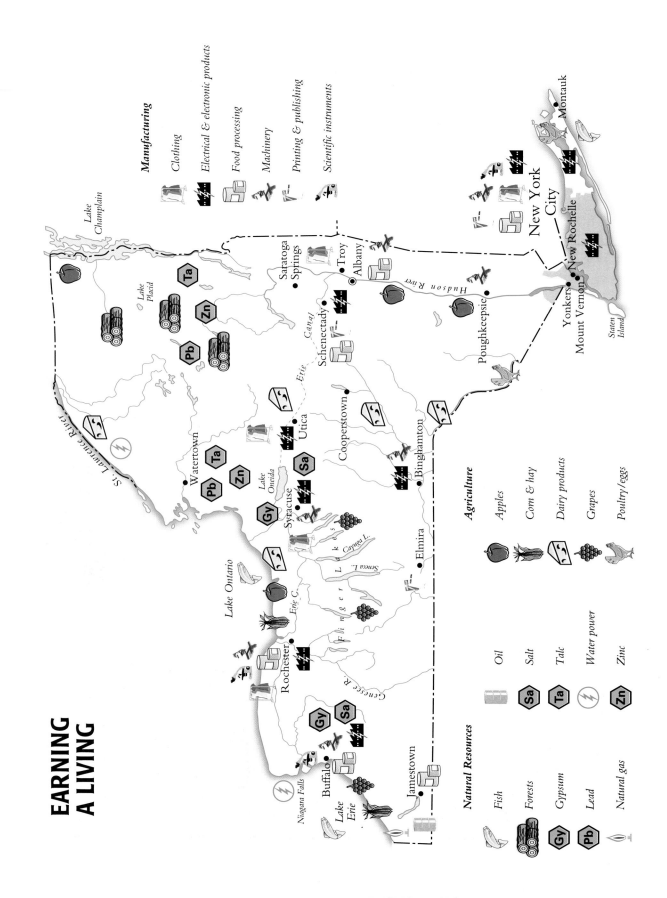

EARNING A LIVING

Manufacturing

Clothing
Electrical & electronic products
Food processing
Machinery
Printing & publishing
Scientific instruments

Agriculture

Apples
Corn & hay
Dairy products
Grapes
Poultry/eggs

Natural Resources

Fish
Forests
Gypsum
Lead
Natural gas
Oil
Salt
Talc
Water power
Zinc

CELEBRATING NATURE'S BOUNTY

Sample a maple lollipop. Dig into a strawberry pizza. Join a grape-stomping contest or try to top the Oyster Bay Festival record for raw oyster eating—two hundred in two minutes and forty seconds. In hundreds of county fairs and local festivals, New Yorkers celebrate nature's riches and the joys of harvest season.

The whole village of Marathon turns out in late March to lend a hand at the Central New York Maple Festival. Villagers tap the local maple trees, boil down the sap, and cook up pancake breakfasts and maple candy, cakes, and cookies.

Farther south, in Owego, the strawberries ripen in June. Music, parades, fireworks, and, of course, lots of pink desserts highlight the Owego Strawberry Festival.

Fall is apple harvest time. New York celebrates its favorite fruit with weekend festivals in dozens of towns and villages. Country clog dancers, old-time fiddlers, storytelling, and hayrides are all part of the entertainment. So are baking contests. At Endicott's Apple Fest a couple of years ago, the world's biggest apple strudel—one hundred feet long—was served to hundreds of apple fans.

Pumpkin painters welcome the fall at the Bleheim Harvest Festival in central New York.

With all its industries, western New York still has room for agriculture. Farmers raise hogs, sheep, and cattle. The flat plains warmed by Lake Erie hold cornfields and hayfields and tangling vines heavy with grapes. Also perfect for grape growing and wine making are the gently sloping shores of the Finger Lakes.

Central and northern New York produce much of America's milk. Many dairy farmers work the same fields their grandparents cleared from forestland. From sunrise to sunset, they tend their growing field grains and feed and milk herds of gentle dairy cows. In some areas, overfarming is using up the fertile topsoil. Harry Nye's father and grandfather owned a two-hundred-acre dairy farm in central New York. "Growing up so close to nature gave me an

*"In the field, a farmer can pick out any cow by name," says Peter K. Mitchell,
a writer from the upstate village of Cazenovia. "He knows which cows . . . are
not feeling well and which feel ill at ease with visitors."*

A mountain lake in the Adirondacks. New York artist Thomas Cole painted these mountains over and over again, trying to capture the " . . . silent energy of nature [that] stirred the soul to its innermost depths."

appreciation for the beauty of this region," he says. "In 1959, the farm was declining, mostly due to poor soil. . . . The animals were sold, and the property began the long process of returning to forest."

In the Adirondacks, the soil was always too thin and rocky for farming. Sometimes the rocks themselves have proved valuable. One Adirondack mine is the country's only source of wollastonite, a mineral used in car brakes. Logging is also an important industry. Mining and logging are forbidden, though, in Adirondack State Park. Over 6 million acres of forests, streams, and lakes have been set aside as protected parkland. This wilderness playground is the reason behind the Adirondacks' number-one business—tourism.

Natural and man-made wonders draw tourists to other parts of the state, too—to Niagara Falls, to the Finger Lakes and Catskill Mountains, and to the famous sites of New York City. New York also touches the lives of millions of people who will never set foot in the state. Products made in New York flow throughout the world. New York City alone produces more goods and services than many countries. The New York Stock Exchange, in the city's Wall Street district, is the economic center of the globe. Millions of dollars' worth of shares in companies worldwide are bought and sold on the Exchange each day.

"When Wall Street sneezes," an old saying goes, "the world catches a cold." That saying reflects an even larger truth. As one of America's business powerhouses, New York plays a central role in the economic health of the world.

4 LIVING TOGETHER

This is New York: The street-smart city dweller, eyes bright, words tumbling, feet flying; the dairy farmer tending a newborn calf, hands strong but gentle and knowing; the class of sixth graders studying spelling words in a language once foreign to many of their parents.

No state has a greater variety of people than New York. Practically every ethnic group and nationality are part of the population mix. About three-quarters of all New Yorkers are white, with families from Germany, Ireland, Italy, Poland, Greece, and other lands. There are over two and a half million African Americans, more than in any other state. New York is home to 2.2 million Hispanics, with roots in Spanish-speaking lands; about 700,000 Asian Americans; and over 60,000 Native Americans. People of every faith live in the state, including one-sixth of the Jews and one-tenth of the Roman Catholics in the United States.

Because of this jumble of backgrounds, there is no such thing as a typical New Yorker. People from different cultures have kept some of their old traditions while absorbing new customs and beliefs. At times, there are tensions between different races, groups, and regions. Overall, though, New Yorkers have an unusual tolerance for different ways of life. "Somehow or other," said former New York City mayor Ed Koch, "we have learned to live with each other."

ETHNIC "SALAD"

Many immigrants making a home in New York have settled among their own kind, in their own separate communities. Having neighbors with the same language and background made them feel more comfortable in an unfamiliar land. Fifty years ago, in many immigrant towns and villages throughout the state, German, Italian, Polish, Greek, and other languages were spoken more often than English. Even today, many different languages can be heard in Manhattan neighborhoods with names like Little Italy and Little Ukraine.

Manhattan's Lower East Side neighborhood was home to over three hundred thousand Jewish immigrants in the early 1900s.

An Orthodox Jew visits a religious articles shop on Manhattan's Lower East Side. Most shops in the neighborhood close from Friday afternoon to Sunday morning in honor of the Jewish sabbath.

OLD-TIME TALES

Many of the traditional tales of New York State are tall tales—exaggerated stories about the adventures of local heroes. In Saratoga County, north of Albany, old-timers still tell tales about a famous local lumberman named Bill Greenfield. Bill was a real person, born in 1833, and it seems he was pretty much responsible for his own fame. He liked to make up adventures starring himself as the hero. Many of his tales were borrowed from old stories told by his Scottish grandfather.

Bill was a big man, the stories say, and he had a BIG appetite. When the lumber camp's cook couldn't make enough pancakes to satisfy him, Bill had a new griddle built that was 235 feet wide. To grease the giant pan, men strapped slabs of bacon on their feet and skated across its surface.

Even the weather around Bill was remarkable. One winter, it was so cold he had to pound the frozen air into pieces just to breathe it. When he built a fire, the flames froze in a column forty feet high. Bill and his father hid out in a cave, but when they tried to talk, their words just froze. The next Fourth of July, Bill returned to the same cave alone and was surprised to hear his dad's voice, just thawing out, saying, "Here, Bill, have a drink."

Lately, shop names and notices in Hebrew have been joined by Spanish and Chinese signs, reflecting the changing face of this community.

New York still has neighborhoods made up mainly of one nationality or ethnic group. Today, though, most New Yorkers live in communities where people with different backgrounds are mixed together like ingredients in a giant salad bowl. Each group is part of the whole colorful concoction, but each adds its own special "flavor."

Cities and neighborhoods show their unique character in the foods and festivals brought by immigrants from their homelands. Shops in Buffalo serve up delicious Polish kielbasa sausage and smoked hams. In Germantown, North Creek, and other towns, German New Yorkers celebrate their heritage with Oktoberfests. These traditional German festivals feature folk dancing, German oompah bands, and plenty of knockwurst and sauerkraut.

In Brooklyn, Italians honor the Feast of Saint Paulinus of Nola

Young Italian Americans wear their heritage with pride for Manhattan's Columbus Day parade.

Bulgarian-American folk dancers bring an ancient tradition to modern New York City.

HAROSET BALLS WITH APPLE

Haroset is a traditional food served during the Jewish festival of Passover. Immigrants from Spain brought this recipe for haroset to New York three hundred years ago. Dates were used in the original recipe. In New York, apples made the perfect substitute.

1. Put 3 cups raisins and 1-1/2 cups blanched almonds in a bowl. Chop them into tiny pieces.*
2. Peel 1/2 apple, remove the core, and add the apple to the raisins and almonds.
3. Add 1/2 teaspoon cinnamon.
4. Finely chop the mixture to make a lumpy paste.
5. Shape the paste into balls about the size of large marbles.
6. Press one whole blanched almond into the top of each haroset ball.

Makes about 48 haroset balls
**When you use sharp knives, ask an adult to help.*

the same way their cousins in Nola, Italy, do. Men dance through the streets carrying the *giglio* (JEEL-yo), a tower holding the saint's statue *plus* a complete orchestra. The Welsh Barn Festival, in Remsen, features the *Gymanfu Ganu,* or Welsh hymnfest, with performances by church choirs. In Altamont, outside Albany, Scots march during the yearly Capital District Scottish Games, wearing the kilts and colors of their ancient family clans.

BLACK CULTURE AND CONFLICTS

Many African-American New Yorkers make their homes in small towns and villages. Most, though, live in the cities, with about three-quarters of New York's African Americans living in New York City.

When southern black immigrants came to New York in the mid-1900s, they found jobs in New York City and other major manufacturing centers, such as Buffalo and Rochester. Large black communities grew up in Brooklyn and in the northern tip of

New Yorkers have their roots in many lands. These young people are celebrating their heritage at the West Indian Caribbean American Carnival in Brooklyn.

Children play in a vacant lot. Writer James Baldwin called the Harlem slums where he grew up " . . . wide, filthy, hostile."

Manhattan, known as Harlem. In the 1920s, Harlem was an exciting place, a center of culture and entertainment. During this period, known as the Harlem Renaissance, thousands admired works by black writers and composers. People came from miles around to Harlem's theaters and nightclubs to enjoy performances by great black actors, singers, and jazz orchestras.

The Harlem Renaissance faded with the Great Depression. After World War II, blacks in Harlem and other city neighborhoods were hit hard by job and housing shortages. Many whites began moving out of the cities to the suburbs—communities on the cities' fringes. As whites moved out of the cities, many poor blacks moved in, filling low-income housing projects built in mostly black neighborhoods.

Yusef Hawkins' murder set off confrontations between blacks and whites all over New York City.

Today parts of Harlem are still lively, with busy clubs, theaters, churches, and restaurants. But much of the community is haunted by unemployment, poverty, crime, and drugs. Writer James Baldwin described Harlem as a sad and dangerous place where "the buildings are old and in desperate need of repair, the streets are crowded and dirty." The people of these crowded streets and of other black city neighborhoods feel angry and frustrated, with little hope for the future.

Anger and tensions between blacks and whites sometimes lead

to violence. In 1989, black teenager Yusef Hawkins was attacked and killed by a gang of young white men in Brooklyn. Blacks rioted in protest, attacking news reporters and police. "This will let the city know that there are young black people who will not take this anymore," said black community leader Sonny Carson.

Later that year, David Dinkins became New York City's first black mayor. Dinkins ran for mayor promising to work to heal the conflicts dividing the races and to "bring New York City together."

New York City Mayor David Dinkins, in 1990. Urging New York's different ethnic groups to make peace, Dinkins pledged, "Instead of attacking each other we will attack common enemies like poverty."

CHERISHED HERITAGES

Hispanic New Yorkers come from a rich variety of backgrounds. Their families have immigrated from Puerto Rico, Cuba, the West Indies, Mexico, Colombia, and other Spanish-speaking lands. Like African Americans, Hispanics live mostly in the larger cities. Over 80 percent live in New York City.

Piri Thomas grew up among the "hustles and rackets" of the Manhattan neighborhood called Spanish Harlem. He wrote about the neighborhood's dirt and noise, the "crying kids, hustlers, dogs yapping, and cats making holes in mountains of garbage." Crime, unemployment, and poverty are serious problems in Spanish Harlem and other Hispanic neighborhoods. Parents who came to the United States hoping to make a better life for their families often cannot find good jobs or housing. They worry when their children see gang violence and drug dealing on the streets.

ETHNIC NEW YORK

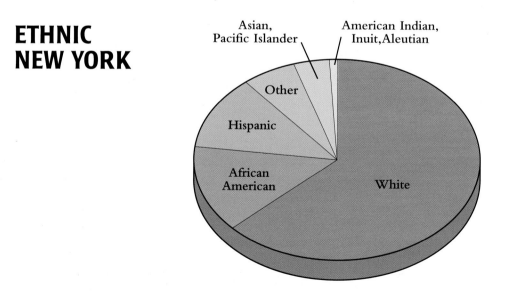

These parents cherish their Spanish heritage and want their children to share their pride in their homeland. Most families visit relatives back home whenever they can. In their New York neighborhoods, they surround themselves with Hispanic clubs, movie houses, radio stations, restaurants, and shops.

La Marqueta is a big, lively marketplace in Spanish Harlem. Its market tables hold colorful mounds of avocados, papayas, and other fruits and vegetables from Spanish lands. Also sold are small statues of Catholic saints. About half of New York's Roman Catholics are Hispanic. Churches in Spanish Harlem come alive

Wearing Boys Club of New York uniforms and displaying the Puerto Rican flag, these Little Leaguers bring ethnic pride to the Lower East Side.

each Sunday morning as families dressed in colorful fashions gather to worship together.

Like Hispanics, most Asian Americans came to the United States in search of a better life for their families. In recent years, people from China, Korea, Japan, the Philippines, and other Asian countries have been New York's fastest-growing immigrant group. In their homelands, these people were taught that nothing is more important than responsibility to family. They have worked hard in New York to give their children a comfortable home and first-rate education.

Korean Americans in New York City have opened thousands of busy groceries and other small stores, often in black neighborhoods. Their success sometimes causes bad feelings between the races. Some Korean storekeepers don't trust their black customers; some blacks refuse to shop in Korean stores. "We need to understand the black people better," says Korean businessman Michael Lee. "I don't want to hurt other people and I don't want to get hurt."

Another problem faced by Asian Americans is gang violence. Some young people roam with gangs that rob stores or make store owners pay "protection" money to avoid being robbed. William Nevins, a police expert on Asian gangs, describes them as "hardcore guys. . . . Five KP [Korean Power gang] guys beat a guy up in his store just recently. They told him that if he had security [protection], this wouldn't happen."

Manhattan's largest Asian neighborhood is Chinatown, home to thousands of Chinese Americans. Colorful banners stretch across Chinatown's narrow, winding streets. Tourists flock to the

Korean Americans line Broadway in New York City to watch their fellow New Yorkers parade.

shops for bargains on everything from teapots to chopsticks to Kung Fu swords. On Chinese New Year, Chinatown's main street overflows with Chinese New Yorkers in colorful costumes, celebrating in a shower of fireworks.

At events such as the Seneca Indian Fall Festival, New York's Native Americans celebrate their heritage with traditional ceremonies, food, dress, and dance. Many Native Americans from tribes including the Seneca, Mohawk, Onondaga, and Oneida live

The Chinese New Year parade in Chinatown is a spectacle of lights, colors, bright banners, and fanciful costumes.

on New York's eight Indian reservations as well as in the large cities. Reservations are lands that were set apart in the late 1700s by the new American government as unfair treaties forced Native Americans off their ancient lands. Today most reservations struggle with poverty, unemployment, and overcrowding. At the Seneca reservation at Tonawanda, Chief Corbett Sundown calls his community "rich people without any money." When white people say the Indians need more industries, Chief Sundown answers, "How're you going to grow potatoes and sweet corn on concrete? You call that progress? To me, 'progress' is a dirty word."

UPSTATE VS. DOWNSTATE

As great as the differences among New York's ethnic groups may seem, there's an even wider gap dividing New Yorkers. That's the gap between people from the regions known as upstate and downstate. No set line on a map defines those regions. To most people, *upstate* means any area outside New York City and its suburbs; the city and nearby communities, including Long Island and the lower Hudson Valley, are *downstate*.

The downstate region has a larger population, including more low-income people who depend on social services. Downstate is home to most of New York's blacks, Hispanics, and Jews. Most upstaters are white and Christian. They may think of downstaters as "different," and they may suspect that downstate gets more than its fair share of federal and state dollars.

In 1982, New York City Mayor Ed Koch stirred up the conflicts between the two regions when he called country living "wasting

TEN LARGEST CITIES

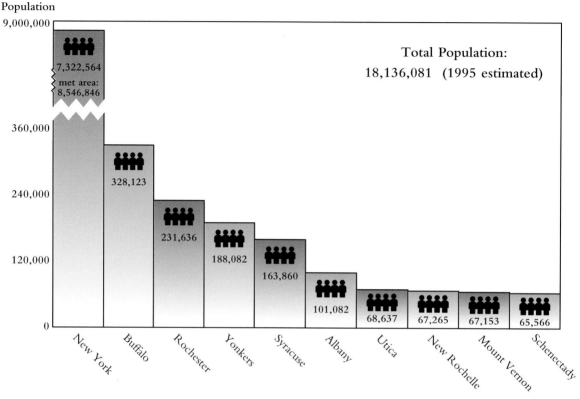

Population

9,000,000

7,322,564
met area:
8,546,846

360,000

328,123

240,000

231,636

188,082

120,000

163,860

101,082

68,637   67,265   67,153   65,566

0

New York   Buffalo   Rochester   Yonkers   Syracuse   Albany   Utica   New Rochelle   Mount Vernon   Schenectady

Total Population:
18,136,081   (1995 estimated)

time in a pickup truck." Burt Phillips of upstate Sackets Harbor responded with a local joke: "The best thing about New York City is the train out."

In recent years, many black, Hispanic, and Asian New Yorkers have moved north, bringing greater ethnic variety to upstate towns and cities. At the same time, thousands of New Yorkers, both upstate and downstate, have moved from cities and farm towns to the growing suburbs. As people from different backgrounds and ethnic groups come together, the sharp line dividing upstate and downstate has begun to soften.

"New York is not a finished culture," wrote historian David Ellis. "It is one continually coming into being." Hardworking people have brought the charm and culture of many lands to New York. The challenges of putting all their different talents to work and learning to live together make New York an exciting, ever-changing state.

5 NOTABLE NEW YORKERS

Many New Yorkers have educated and entertained us. Others have worked to make life better for all Americans. Here are just a few of the many people of New York State who have made their mark on the nation and the world.

SLEEPY HOLLOW DREAMS

Born in New York City five days after the close of the American Revolution, Washington Irving grew up to become the new nation's first great writer. "Of all the scenery of the Hudson," he said, "the Caatskill mountains had the most witching effect on my boyish imagination." That "witching effect" and the legends Irving heard as a boy found their way into the writer's comical tales about New York's early Dutch settlers.

In "Rip Van Winkle," a lazy, good-natured fellow falls under a spell and takes a twenty-year nap among the magical Catskills. In "The Legend of Sleepy Hollow," gangly schoolmaster Ichabod Crane visits the little Dutch village of Tarrytown, a "pleasing land of drowsy head" also known as Sleepy Hollow. After hearing one too many stories about local ghosts and goblins, Ichabod is chased by a dark figure that he fears is the legendary "headless horseman."

Washington Irving built his home in Sleepy Hollow country, on the banks of the Hudson River. His magnificent front lawn, he proudly wrote, was "the most delicious bank in the world for Dozing, Dreaming and Reading."

MANHATTAN'S SON

> Brooklyn of ample hills was mine,
> I too walked the streets of Manhattan island,
> and bathed in the waters around it, . . .

Born on Long Island and raised in Brooklyn, Walt Whitman often turned to New York's sights and sounds for inspiration in his writings. One of America's most celebrated poets, Whitman called himself a "son of Manhattan." "Tides swift and ample, well-loved by me," he wrote of his beloved hometown. "City of hurried and sparkling waters! City of spires and masts! . . . my city!"

During the Civil War, Whitman nursed wounded soldiers in war hospitals, holding their hands and listening to their stories. He wept for the "young men once so handsome and so joyous, taken from us—the son from the mother, the husband from the wife, the dear friend from the dear friend." Whitman admired Abraham Lincoln and was stunned when the president was assassinated five days after the war's end. One of his best-known poems honored the president's memory:

> When lilacs last in the dooryard bloom'd,
> And the great star early droop'd in the western sky in the night,
> I mourn'd, and yet shall mourn with ever-returning spring. . . .

I HEAR AMERICA SINGING

Walt Whitman's poetry, written in a bold new style of rhythmic, nonrhyming verse, celebrated American democracy, the worth of each individual, and the beauty of the human body.

I hear America singing, the varied carols I hear,
Those of mechanics, each one singing his as it should be blithe and strong,
The carpenter singing his as he measures his plank or beam,
The mason singing his as he makes ready for work, or leaves off work,
The boatman singing what belongs to him in his boat, the deck-hand
    singing on the steamboat deck,
The shoemaker singing as he sits on his bench, the hatter singing as he
    stands,
The wood-cutter's song, the ploughboy's on his way in the morning,
    or at noon intermission or at sundown,
The delicious singing of the mother, or of the young wife at work,
    or of the girl sewing or washing,
Each singing what belongs to him or her and to none else,
The day what belongs to the day—at night the party of young fellows,
    robust, friendly,
    Singing with open mouths their strong melodious songs.

—Walt Whitman (1860)

VOICE FOR FREEDOM

Growing up in the slums of Harlem, James Baldwin dreamed of "a big Buick car, and I was driving it. . . . I'd drive up my block and everyone would notice me. My family would be so proud of their rich and famous son."

Baldwin's novels, essays, and plays did make him rich and famous. His powerful writings drew on his experiences as a child living poor and hungry in a "wide, filthy, hostile" ghetto, among "wine-stained and urine-splashed hallways" and windows "like a

James Baldwin's novels, plays, and essays exposed the harsh realities of racism in America.

thousand blinded eyes." Even after he achieved fame, Baldwin found that many stores and restaurants closed their doors to him because he was black. In 1948, disgusted with American racism, the author moved to Europe.

Baldwin returned home in the 1950s to lend his voice to the American civil rights struggle. His essays exploring black-white relations in the United States opened many people's eyes to the brutality of racism.

THE BIG APPLE ON THE BIG SCREEN

"I'm not a smiler," Woody Allen admits. "If you didn't know I was a comic, I would be a study in sadness." In the 1960s, Allen's sad-sack looks helped him build a successful career as a nightclub comedian. Soon he was writing, directing, and often starring in his own plays and movies, playing a luckless fellow who worries about *everything*.

Allen lives in an elegant Manhattan apartment, and the city is the setting for many of his films. *Manhattan,* the story of a New York City comedy writer and his nutty friends, opens with sweeping scenes of crowded streets and glamorous high-rises. In *Annie Hall*, Woody plays comedian Alvy Singer, who claims he "was brought up underneath the roller coaster in the Coney Island section of Brooklyn. Maybe that accounts for my personality, which is a little nervous." Alvy loves Annie Hall but loses her when she moves from his beloved New York to California. "You want to live out here?" he asks in disbelief. "It's like living in Munchkin land."

Most of Allen's movies are comedies, but recent films have mixed

Woody Allen says he started making serious films because, "When you do comedy, you're not sitting at the grown-ups' table."

humor with a more serious look at life. Director Spike Lee has always tackled serious subjects in his films, driven by a mission to "put the vast richness of black culture on film."

Lee grew up in a mostly black section of Brooklyn, a neighborhood he has brought to the screen in movies including *Do the Right Thing* and *Crooklyn*. A racial incident in Queens inspired the making of *Do the Right Thing*. In 1986, three black men whose car broke down in a white neighborhood were chased and beaten by

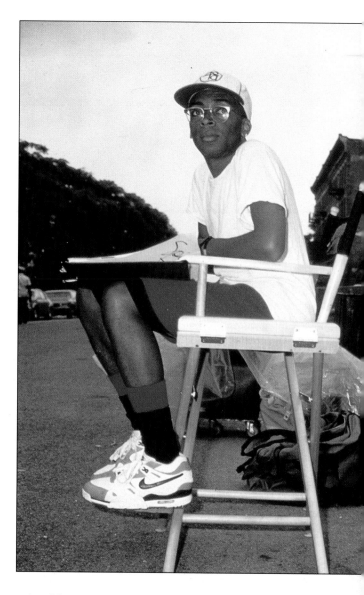

a crowd of white youths. Lee's film examines "not only the people who are the recipients of [racism], but the people who are handing it out." *Crooklyn* is "very, very loosely based" on the film-maker's memories of his Brooklyn childhood. The movie shows "a normal family who fight and fuss and love."

Some people say Spike Lee has worked a revolution in the way blacks are shown in American films. Others call him a trouble-maker. "When white people stand up for their rights, they [are] freedom fighters," he responds, "but if a black man gets up and speaks for his rights, he's militant!"

SPORTS SUPERSTARS

Talented athletes on state baseball, football, hockey, and basketball teams have made sports fans of many New Yorkers. No team has had a more exciting history than baseball's New York Yankees. Famous Yankee players have included Babe Ruth, Joe DiMaggio,

New York Yankee great Babe Ruth belts a high one.

Mickey Mantle, and Reggie Jackson. First baseman Lou Gehrig earned the nickname "The Iron Horse." In 1939, the native New Yorker played his 2,130th game in a row, setting a record unbeaten for fifty-six years. Gehrig claimed he couldn't take a rest because "I like to play baseball, and if I were to sit on the bench . . . the worrying and fretting would take too much out of me."

Basketball is number one on many of New York's neighborhood ball courts and playgrounds. Kareem Abdul-Jabbar grew up practicing hook shots on city courts. In high school, as "the second tallest guy in the school," he was automatically on the basketball team but thought himself "too timid, skinny, and nowhere near good enough."

The high-flying athlete went on to a spectacular twenty-year career with the National Basketball Association. Fans loved his "skyhook," an arching overhand shot that basketball great Bill Russell called "the most beautiful thing in sports." In 1984, Abdul-Jabbar scored his 38,387th point, breaking the NBA all-time scoring record. He grinned as "the fans went wild, the officials stopped the game and gave me the ball. My mother and father came on the court. It was a wonderful moment."

LEADING THE WAY

Many New Yorkers have led battles for human rights. As First Lady to President Franklin D. Roosevelt and for many years after his death, Eleanor Roosevelt worked tirelessly for better conditions for the poor and minorities. Journalist Frank Kingdon recalled touring a poverty-stricken coal-mining town during the Great

Elizabeth Cady Stanton fought for women's rights, especially the right to vote. "I say clearly," she said, "that the power to make the laws was the right through which all other rights could be secured."

Depression. In a tiny hut, he was astonished to find Eleanor Roosevelt, sitting on a cot, holding a sickly baby while the mother stirred a pot of thin soup. "The two women were discussing their household problems as though that . . . hut were no different from a Washington drawing room."

Another famous champion of human rights was Elizabeth Cady

Stanton. Studying in her father's law office, Stanton learned about laws that denied women equal rights with men. In 1848, in Seneca Falls, she organized America's first women's rights convention, with the goal of solving "the wrongs of society in general, and of women in particular." She and other reformers fought for laws that gave women control of their money and property. Stanton died before victory was won in her greatest battle. In 1995, New Yorkers celebrated that victory with the "75 in '95" festival in Seneca Falls. The festival marked the seventy-fifth anniversary of the 19th Amendment to the U.S. Constitution, which gave women the right to vote.

AN AMERICAN JOURNEY

Colin Powell grew up in the South Bronx, where people kept their "doors and windows locked. Burglaries were common. Drug use was on the rise. Street fighting and knifings occurred." Powell's mother and father, immigrants from the Caribbean country of Jamaica, ruled their home with a firm but loving hand. "My mother [could] snap me back in line with a simple rebuke: 'I'm ashamed of you. You've embarrassed the family,'" he recalls. "I would have preferred a beating to hearing those words."

Through long hours of hard work in New York City's clothing factories, Powell's parents earned enough to send the son they called "Sweet Pea" to college. After graduating, Powell joined the army. He rose to become a four-star general. In 1989, he was named the first black chairman of the Joint Chiefs of Staff, the nation's top military post.

Many people hoped that Colin Powell would run for president in 1996, but the retired general announced that, " . . . [becoming] a candidate for president requires . . . a passion and commitment that, despite my every effort, I do not have for the political life."

In 1995, the retired general told about his life in a book called *My American Journey*. "We have to start thinking of America as a family," he wrote. "My responsibility, our responsibility as lucky Americans, is to try to give back to this country as much as it has given to us, as we continue our American journey together."

6 EXPLORING NEW YORK

New York has it all—soaring skyscrapers, world-class museums, majestic waterways, unspoiled wilderness. Let's take a trip around the state and explore some of its many wonders.

THE NORTH COUNTRY

Our journey begins in a leaf-carpeted forest. An hour's hike leads to a view of deep green hills and pools that sparkle like diamonds. Around us stretch 6 million acres of forests, mountains, lakes, and river valleys. We are in Adirondack Park, a northern wilderness as big as the state of Vermont.

Nearly half of the Adirondacks is owned by the state and set aside to remain "forever wild." Scattered throughout these wild, untouched lands is property owned by people who have built campgrounds, ski resorts, and small towns. This unusual mix of wilderness and civilization shows New York's commitment to preserving its natural wonders while opening up opportunities to its citizens.

Whiteface Mountain is an example of that commitment. The highest skiing peak in the East, Whiteface is the Adirondack's only high peak reachable by car (the others must be hiked). In 1935, President Franklin Roosevelt opened the new state highway to the

PLACES TO SEE

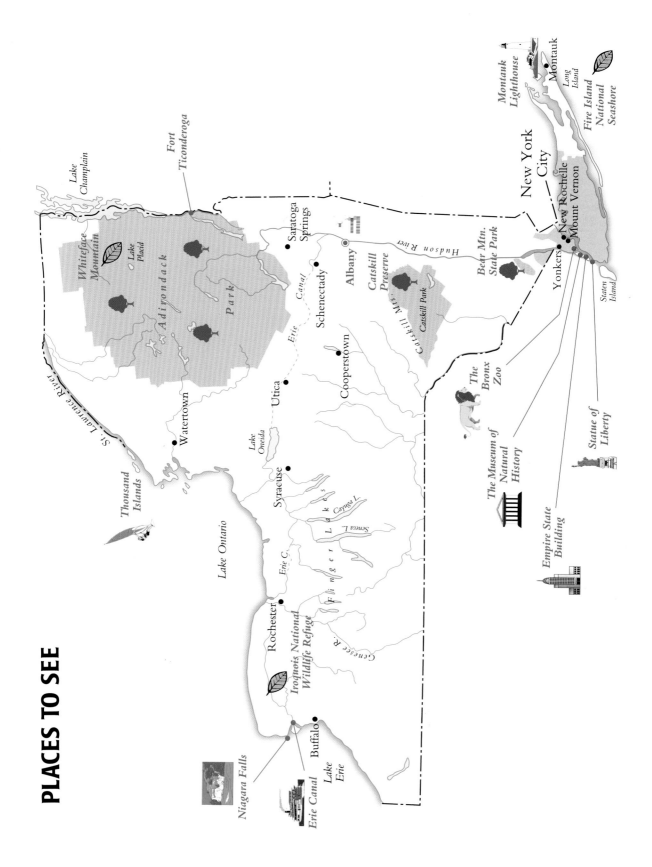

Montauk Lighthouse

Montauk

Long Island

Fire Island National Seashore

Lake Champlain

Fort Ticonderoga

New York City

New Rochelle

Mount Vernon

Whiteface Mountain

Lake Placid

Saratoga Springs

Albany

Bear Mtn. State Park

Adirondack

Park

Erie Canal

Schenectady

Catskill Preserve

Catskill Mts

Catskill Park

Yonkers

Staten Island

St. Lawrence River

Watertown

Cooperstown

Utica

Lake Oneida

The Bronx Zoo

The Museum of Natural History

Thousand Islands

Syracuse

Finger Lakes

Cayuga L.

Seneca L.

Empire State Building

Statue of Liberty

Lake Ontario

Erie C.

Genesee R.

Rochester

Iroquois National Wildlife Refuge

Niagara Falls

Erie Canal

Buffalo

Lake Erie

CELEBRATING THE NORTH COUNTRY

North Country New Yorkers take special pride in their wild, beautiful region. Each August, in Massena, in the Saint Lawrence Valley, that pride shines at the Festival of North Country Folklife. Banjo players and fiddlers play old songs from the logging camps. Craftspeople demonstrate Adirondack furniture making, rug weaving, and decoy carving. The smell of hearty French-Canadian meat pies and pea soup beckons from the food tent. The Talker's Tent serves up another North Country specialty. There old-timers tell outrageous stories about loggers, hunters, and guides whose adventures are part of the treasury of Adirondack tall tales.

mountaintop. "Many persons cannot indulge in the luxury of camping or climbing," Roosevelt said. "We have now got the means for their coming up here on four wheels."

In the shadow of Whiteface lies Lake Placid, site of the 1932 and 1980 Winter Olympic games. The young men and women jogging through this famous lakeside ski town are athletes training for the next Olympics.

Farther north, on Lake Champlain, we come to Ausable Chasm. Five hundred million years ago, the Ausable River carved this deep path through sandstone. If you're adventurous, we can take a wild ride down the rapids that tumble between the one-hundred-foot-high cliff walls.

Fort Ticonderoga guards Lake Champlain's southern end. Built by the French in 1755, the fort was captured by the British and then by American Revolutionary forces. This bit of colonial history lives on in the red-coated soldiers who patrol the fort grounds and fire the mighty cannons.

West of the Adirondacks, the Thousand Islands dot the lower Saint Lawrence River. Some of these rocky islands stretch over twenty miles, while others measure just a few feet. One of the most interesting is Heart Island. In 1900, millionaire George Boldt began building a 120-room stone-and-marble castle here for his beloved wife, Louise. When Louise suddenly died, all work halted. Today half-finished Boldt Castle is a reminder of wealth and lost dreams.

WESTERN NEW YORK

From the Thousand Islands, the scenic Seaway Trail leads west along Lake Ontario to the Niagara River and awesome Niagara Falls. Few wonders can match the sight and sound of seven hundred thousand gallons of water per second crashing down a 167-foot rock ledge. Daredevils have been challenging the falls for over a century. In 1859, French tightrope walker the Great Blondin walked across on a three-inch-wide rope, carrying his terrified manager on his shoulders. Others have taken the plunge in boats, rubber tubes, and barrels. We can get a close-up look in safer ways. There are walkways beside the falls, helicopter tours, and boat rides through the mist and spray at the base.

The Finger Lakes region has its own glittering waterfalls, including Taughannock Falls, higher even than Niagara. There are also thousands of acres of protected parkland in western New York, plus nature preserves filled with wild plants and animals. In Iroquois

The Merwin family poses for an 1880 photo on the porch of their hotel, where the Adirondack Museum now stands.

More than 10 million visitors a year come to marvel at the great falls that Native Americans named "Niagara—thunder of the waters."

National Wildlife Refuge, two hundred types of birds nest in marshland beside Cayuga, Seneca, Onondaga, Oneida, and Mohawk Pools. In Letchworth State Park, the Genesee River cuts a seventeen-mile-long canyon through towering rock walls. Nearby a statue of a tall woman with braided hair marks the grave of Mary Jemison, the "white woman of the Genesee." Captured by a Native American war party at age fifteen, Jemison lived a long, happy life as a Seneca.

The west's big cities hold man-made treasures. Buffalo is known for its fine architecture. The Guaranty Building has been called the greatest American skyscraper, and there are five homes designed by famous architect Frank Lloyd Wright. Rochester has great museums. In the fifty-room mansion of inventor George Eastman, the history of photography is told through pictures and hands-on displays. In Corning, we can watch skilled craftspeople at the Steuben Factory transform hot liquid glass into delicate crystal.

CENTRAL NEW YORK

For a relaxed crossing from Lake Erie to central New York, we might rent a houseboat and cruise the historic Erie Canal. The 801-mile waterway wanders past small towns and stone bridges. Along the way, our boat passes through fifty-seven canal locks. The largest is at Lockport. After we float into the lock's holding chamber, the tenders gently lower us sixty feet to the next water level.

There's much to see once we reach Albany. A stroll takes us past historic buildings and modern architectural marvels. Blockhouse Church, first built by the Dutch in 1616, once guarded the Hudson with cannons mounted in its balcony. Up the hill is the gleaming Empire State Plaza, built by Governor Nelson Rockefeller in the 1970s. The plaza's eleven marble and glass buildings include a performing arts center, an observation tower, and the New York State Museum. At the museum, exhibits called dioramas, with realistic models and scenery, give us a chapter-by-chapter view of New York's history. The most magnificent plaza building is the New York State Capitol. This $25 million granite extravaganza took more than thirty years to build and looks like a huge French castle.

Just north of Albany is Saratoga Springs. Horse racing and the arts are this popular resort town's main attractions. Until recently, most people came to relax in the thick-smelling mineral springs, which were believed to cure illness. A few miles east of town, a winding stairway leads to the top of Saratoga Monument. This 155-foot-tall tower marks the Revolutionary War battlefield where in 1777 Americans claimed their first victory over a British army.

After Saratoga, central New York's most famous spot is Cooperstown. An old story says Abner Doubleday invented baseball here. Whether that's true or not, the village is the site of the National Baseball Hall of Fame and Museum, dedicated to the game and its players.

THE HUDSON VALLEY

It's back to our houseboat for a cruise down the Hudson. The journey from Albany to New York Harbor will take us past towering cliffs, picture-postcard towns, and million-dollar mansions.

Our first stop is Hyde Park. Here we can visit the home of

Top thoroughbreds race at Saratoga Race Course, the oldest flat track in the nation.

Franklin D. Roosevelt. It feels like we've taken a step back in time as we walk through the president's house, left exactly as it was the day he died. Across town is Vanderbilt Mansion. Millionaire Frederick Vanderbilt shipped in craftspeople from Europe to create this spectacular fifty-room palace. Further down the river, Boscobel mansion is a masterpiece of the style of architecture called Federal, popular following the Revolutionary War. In the 1950s, Boscobel was torn apart. A group of local residents bought the pieces from the wrecking crew and kept them in their garages until money could be raised to restore the building.

From Boscobel's garden, we spot West Point, across the Hudson. The U.S. Military Academy at West Point trains young people to

Cadets parade at West Point, training ground for top United States Army officers.

Vanderbilt Museum is a dazzling example of the fabulous lifestyles of New York's Gilded Age millionaires.

become U.S. Army officers. The first fort on this site was built by American colonists during the Revolution, on a "point west" of advancing British troops.

Bear Mountain State Park is the survivor of a different kind of conflict. In the early 1900s, New Yorkers were outraged by a state plan to build a prison on this beautiful, wild chunk of shoreline.

A wealthy woman, Mary Harriman, put an end to the plan by offering the state $1 million to turn the area into a park instead. A larger-than-life statue of Walt Whitman, poet of New York's wonders, was placed in the park in Harriman's honor.

The lower Hudson Valley is Sleepy Hollow country, made famous by the stories of Washington Irving. Sunnyside, Irving's home in Tarrytown, is a charming cottage that looks like something straight from the pages of a fairy tale.

A short side trip west takes us to the Catskill Mountains, the "fairy mountains" where Irving's Rip Van Winkle slept away twenty years. The Catskill region is a paradise of crystal lakes and fresh mountain streams. Catskill Preserve includes 135,000 acres of protected forestland. The Catskills also are famous for ski resorts and sprawling luxury hotels.

LONG ISLAND

The Hudson meets the Atlantic Ocean at New York Harbor. Let's turn east beneath Manhattan's tall towers and circle around Long Island.

The north shore of the island has been called the "Gold Coast." A string of mansions built by nineteenth-century business tycoons line these wooded shores. Here also is the simple boyhood home of Walt Whitman. Made of hand-cut logs held together by wooden pegs, the poet's five-room farmhouse is a museum filled with reminders of his life.

The tiny south fork village of Sag Harbor once was one of the world's busiest whaling ports. To enter the Whaling Museum, we walk through a giant set of whale's jaws. Inside, exhibits show how New Yorkers hunted whales in the 1800s.

Rounding Long Island's eastern tip, we pass Montauk Lighthouse. This sturdy tower was built in 1795 by order of President George Washington. In those days, it stood two hundred feet from the ocean. Over time, crashing waves have worn away the shoreline. Today the lighthouse shines its beacon just fifty feet from the edge of a cliff.

Our return trip along Long Island's southern shore takes us past mile after mile of ocean beaches. Two long sections are parkland—Fire Island National Seashore and Jones Beach State Park. On summer days, the parks are a perfect place to cool off in ocean waves washing white sand beaches.

NEW YORK CITY

Our journey at last brings us to New York City, America's largest city and one of the most exciting places in the world. Whatever you're looking for, you'll find it here—fantastic skyscrapers, museums, theaters, parks, zoos, beaches, and more.

Jazz musicians in the 1920s nicknamed New York City the "Big Apple." When they played here, they'd really hit the "big time." The apple is divided into five boroughs—Manhattan, Brooklyn, the Bronx, Queens, and Staten Island.

Brooklyn is connected to Manhattan by the Brooklyn Bridge. With its spiderweb of wires, this is often called the most beautiful bridge in the world. Coney Island, on Brooklyn's southern tip, is famous for its three-mile beach and amusement park.

CELEBRATING BROOKLYN

Brooklyn has hundreds of neighborhoods, and most have a strong ethnic character. People from all the neighborhoods mingle with ex-Brooklynites visiting home at the Welcome Back to Brooklyn festival. This summertime street fair begins with a children's parade led by the "King of Brooklyn," a local "graduate" who's gone on to fame. Along the mile-long route are crafts booths and vendors selling ethnic foods. Entertainment is provided by performers from differing backgrounds. Past stars have included Dairaba West Afrikan Dance Company, Young Soon Kim White Wave Rising Dance Company, and the musical group Roots of Brazil.

The magnificent Brooklyn Bridge was one of the great engineering wonders of the nineteenth century. Behind its graceful cables and arches pointing to heaven rise the twin towers of the World Trade Center.

The Bronx has high-rise apartments, housing projects, and America's largest city wildlife park, the Bronx Zoo. Here snow leopards, red pandas, lions, tigers, and bears roam in re-creations of their natural environments.

Queens is crowded with office towers, apartments, factories, and two huge airports. Outside the noisy streets, nearly a quarter of the borough is protected parkland. At Jamaica Bay Wildlife Refuge, we can hike a wilderness trail, surrounded by three hundred types of wild birds and animals.

Staten Island is the least populated of the boroughs. Most Staten Islanders travel by ferryboat to and from jobs in Manhattan. The ride offers terrific views at a bargain price—just 50 cents round-trip.

The smallest borough in size, Manhattan is biggest in just about everything else. Do you like heights? How about a 110-story elevator ride to the top of the World Trade Center? The twin towers of this giant office complex are New York's highest buildings. From the roof of tower 2, we can look down on helicopters, tiny cars and people, all five boroughs, Long Island, and New Jersey.

In the 1930s, the Empire State Building was the world's tallest skyscraper. This 102-story building has a long, thin tower that was designed so passenger blimps could land by tying onto it.

Manhattan's biggest and best museum is the Metropolitan Museum of Art. The Met's more than 3 million exhibits include Egyptian mummies, Joan of Arc's helmet, and an entire room from the home of architect Frank Lloyd Wright. At the American Museum of Natural History, we can inspect moon rocks, a ninety-four-foot stuffed whale, and gigantic dinosaur skeletons. Across town, there's a floating sea, air, and space museum on board the *Intrepid,* a World War II aircraft carrier. Manhattan has more than one hundred other museums of art, science, music, photography, television, different ethnic groups and nationalities—you name it.

We can't visit Manhattan without taking in a play. The most famous theaters are around Broadway, in a six-block stretch known as Times Square. Lincoln Center is a grand complex of buildings devoted to symphony music, opera, and ballet. Radio City Music Hall is America's largest indoor theater. The famous Radio City Rockettes, a line of long-legged dancers, kick to the music before the start of each movie or stage show.

Radio City is just one of nineteen buildings in a twenty-two-acre business and entertainment complex called Rockefeller Center. Built by millionaire John D. Rockefeller, Jr., the center is like a city within a city. More than 240,000 people a day jam its offices, shops, restaurants, movie theaters, and outdoor skating rink. Towering over them all is a golden statue of the ancient Greek god Prometheus.

The World Trade Center towers over lower Manhattan on a moonlit night.

To see a *nation* within a city, we must head for United Nations Headquarters. This building is considered international territory, so when we enter it, we've left the United States. In the Visitors' Gallery, we put on headphones to hear representatives from 185 U.N. member nations discuss how to work together peacefully.

One of the world's greatest symbols of freedom and peace between nations stands in New York Harbor. The Statue of Liberty was a gift from France to the United States. Sculptor Frédéric Auguste Bartholdi shipped the pieces to America in 214 crates. In 1886, the 152-foot copper statue was placed on a pedestal on Liberty Island. For boatloads of European immigrants, the sight of the gleaming lady with the blazing torch meant the end of a long journey to hope and freedom.

Today the Statue of Liberty is a national monument. A museum at its base honors the struggles and contributions of America's immigrants. Standing in Liberty's crown, we look across the harbor to the city those immigrants led to greatness. It's a good place to end our journey, where so many Americans began theirs—at New York Harbor, jewel of the state that is the crown of the nation.

"... *Give me your tired, your poor,*
Your huddled masses yearning to breathe free,
The wretched refuse of your teeming shore,
Send these, the homeless, tempest-tost to me,
I lift my lamp beside the golden door!"
                —*Emma Lazarus*
                  (*from her poem engraved in the*
                  pedestal of the Statue of Liberty)

THE FLAG: *The flag was officially adopted in 1909. It shows the state seal on a dark blue background. New York's seal was first painted on a silk flag for the Third New York Regiment during the American revolution.*

THE SEAL: *Adopted in 1882, the seal shows two women holding a shield. The blindfolded woman represents Justice; the other stands for Liberty. Within the shield are two Hudson River ships with a sun rising over a mountain. The shield is topped by a bald eagle with outstretched wings. The ribbon beneath the women's feet displays the state motto in Latin, Excelsior.*

STATE SURVEY

Statehood: July 26, 1788

Origin of Name: Named to honor England's Duke of York and Albany, who later became King James II

Nickname: The Empire State

Capital: Albany

Motto: Ever Upward

Bird: Bluebird

Animal: Beaver

Fish: Brook trout

Flower: Rose

Tree: Sugar maple

Gem: Garnet

Fruit: Apple

Beverage: Milk

Muffin: Apple muffin

Bluebird

Sugar Maples

THE NEW COLOSSUS

Although many songs have been written in praise of New York, the state has, in fact, no official song. There is one symbol that speaks to all New Yorkers and all other Americans as well: The Statue of Liberty. Emma Lazarus wrote the poem, "The New Colossus," which is inscribed on a tablet at the base of the statue. Jerry Silverman has put her words to music.

Words by Emma Lazarus
Music by Jerry Silverman
(Used by permission)

Not like the bra-zen gi-ant of Greek fame, With con-quer-ing limbs a-stride from land to land,

Here at our sea-washed sun-set gates shall stand A might-ty—wo-man with a torch whose flame is the em-

pris-oned light-ning. And her name Moth-er of Ex-iles. From her bea-con hand glows world-wide

wel-come; her mild— eyes com-mand the air-bridged har-bor that twin cit-ies frame.

"Keep, an-cient lands, your stor-ied pomp!" cried she with si-lent lips. "Give me your tired, your

poor, your hud-dled mass-es yearn-ing to breathe free, The wretch-ed ref-use

of your teem-ing shore. Send these, the home-less, tem-pest-tost to me, I

lift my lamp be-side the gold-en shore.

lift my lamp be-side the gold-en shore.

GEOGRAPHY

Highest Point: Mount Marcy in the Adirondack Mountains—5,344 feet

Lowest Point: Sea level along the Atlantic Coast

Area: 49,108 square miles

Greatest Distance, North to South: 310 miles

Greatest Distance, East to West (including Long Island): 450 miles

Bordering States: Vermont, Massachusetts, and Connecticut to the east, New Jersey and Pennsylvania to the south, a piece of Pennsylvania to the west

Hottest Recorded Temperature: 108° F at Troy on July 22, 1926

Coldest Recorded Temperature: -52° F at Old Forge on February 18, 1979

Average Annual Precipitation: 39 inches

Major Rivers: Hudson, Mohawk, St. Lawrence, Delaware, Black, Genessee, Niagara, Oswego, Susquehanna, Saranac, Ausable

Major Lakes: Erie, Ontario, Champlain, George, Oneida, Seneca, Cayuga, Sacandaga, Canandaigua, Chautauqua, Black, Saranac, Placid

Trees: sugar maple, birch, aspen, oak, elm, hickory, beech, white pine, shortleaf pine, spruce, fir, red cedar, ash, hemlock, laurel, sweet gum, cherry

Wild Plants: rose, bleeding heart, Jacob's-ladder, violet, Indian pipes, Queen Ann's lace, buttercup, daisy, black-eyed Susan, goldenrod, devil's paintbrush, toothwort, bittersweet, dandelion, clover, trillium

Bleeding Heart

Animals: beaver, white-tailed deer, black bear, wildcat, red fox, muskrat, raccoon, skunk, rabbit, chipmunk, squirrel, porcupine, woodchuck, shrew, opposum, wood frog, garden snake, eastern rattlesnake, copperhead

Birds: bluebird, blue jay, cardinal, sparrow, robin, meadowlark, swallow, thrush, chickadee, woodpecker, wren, crow, oriole, plover, rock dove, mourning dove, barn owl, loon, Canada goose, pheasant, partridge, wild duck, wild turkey, bald eagle, peregrine falcon, hawk, gull, tern

Fish: lake trout, rainbow trout, pickerel, pike, perch, sunfish, crappie, bass, salmon, bullhead, flounder, fluke, tuna, blackfish, weakfish, bluefish, stripped bass, swordfish, shad, squid, mussels, lobster

Endangered Animals: Indiana bat, gray wolf, cougar, sperm whale, right whale, finback whale, eastern woodrat, bald eagle, peregrine falcon, least tern, piping plover, eastern sand darter, bog turtle, leatherback turtle, hawksbill sea turtle, round whitefish, shortnose sturgeon, pugnose shiner, deepwater sculpin, karner blue butterfly, dwarf wedge mussel

Endangered Plants: bleeding heart, alpine azalea, small white ladyslipper, Jacob's-ladder, Houghton's goldenrod, coastal violet, silvery aster, Michigan lily, scarlet Indian paintbrush, trailing arbutus, pitcher plant, purple trillium, climbing fern, maidenhair fern, American bittersweet, alpine sweetgrass, northern reed grass, white milkweed, Appalachian firmoss, swamp clubmoss, saltmarsh bulrush, strawberry bush, dwarf blueberry, mountain watercress, mountain laurel, dwarf white birch, dwarf willow, willow oak, Virginia pine

TIMELINE

New York History

1524 Giovanni Verrazano enters New York Harbor

c. 1570 Iroquois League established

1609 Henry Hudson sails up the Hudson River, later named for him

1609 Samuel de Champlain explores around Lake Champlain

1624 Dutch establish settlement at Fort Orange (now Albany)

1664 English take over New Netherland and rename it New York

1734 John Peter Zenger acquitted of libel, laying the foundation for freedom of the press

1754 Albany Congress attempts to unite the colonies

1765 Stamp Act Congress meets in Albany

1775 American Revolution begins; Americans capture Fort Ticonderoga

1776 British capture New York City

1777 Americans win the Battle of Saratoga

1783 American Revolution ends

1785 New York City becomes the nation's capital for five years

1788 New York becomes the eleventh state

1802 West Point Military Academy opens

1807 Steamship Clermont sails up the Hudson from New York City to Albany

1814 British defeated at the Battle of Plattsburg during the War of 1812

1825 The Erie Canal opens, linking the Hudson River to Lake Erie

1827 Slavery is abolished in the state

1831 Mohawk & Hudson Railroad opens

1848 First women's rights convention held in Seneca Falls

1861–1865 United States is torn by the Civil War

1863 New Yorkers riot over Civil War draft laws

1883 The Brooklyn Bridge is completed

1886 The Statue of Liberty is dedicated

1898 Brooklyn, Manhattan, The Bronx, Queens, and Staten Island are united to form Greater New York City

1909 The National Association for the Advancement of Colored People (NAACP) founded in New York City

1911 Fire at the Triangle Shirtwaist Factory kills 146 people and leads to labor reform

1928 New York Barge Canal System opens

1929 Stock Market crashes in New York City; Great Depression Begins

1931 Empire State Building is completed in New York City

1939 New York World's Fair opens in Flushing Meadows in Queens

1946 New York City is chosen as the site of the United Nations

1949 The St. Lawrence Seaway opens

1964 The Verrazano-Narrows Bridge, the world's longest suspension bridge, opens

1980 Lake Placid hosts the Winter Olympic Games

1989 David Dinkins elected New York City's first black mayor

1993 Ruth Bader Ginsburg of Brooklyn is second woman nominated to the Supreme Court

ECONOMY

Natural Resources: fish and shellfish, lumber, granite, sand, emery, gypsum, salt, natural gas, oil, limestone, zinc

Agricultural Products: dairy and beef cattle, pigs, sheep, chickens, ducks, eggs, apples, cherries, grapes, carrots, celery, onions, cabbage, beets, potatoes, corn, honey, maple syrup

Manufacturing: printing materials, scientific instruments, machinery, chemicals, optical equipment, photographic materials, computers, paper, processed food, textiles, glass

Business and Trade: wholesale and retail trade, banking, finance, communications, publishing, advertising, entertainment, tourism

STATE STARS

Bella Abzug (1920–), born in New York City, became a leading figure in the women's liberation movement of the 1960s. As a representative in Congress, she fought hard to see that the city got its fair share of federal money. She once suggested that New York City might become a state. In 1995, Abzug led a group to the women's conference in Beijing, China.

Susan B. Anthony (1820–1906) was one of the foremost leaders of women's struggle for the right to vote. From her home in Rochester, Anthony planned, wrote, and campaigned. Her constant message was "Failure is impossible."

Mariah Carey (1970–), from Huntington, began writing songs as a teenager and knew she wanted to be a singer. In New York City, she got

her big break and began recording. Her first album, *Mariah Carey*, sold 6 million copies and won her two Grammys. Later albums also sold in the millions.

Shirley Chisholm (1924–), born in Brooklyn, was the first black woman to be elected to Congress. In 1972, she became the first African American to run for President on the Democratic ticket. Chisholm went on to become a lecturer and speaker.

Grover Cleveland (1837–1908) of Buffalo served as mayor of that city, governor of New York, and in 1884 was elected President of the United States. Known for his honesty, Cleveland opposed the bosses who ran the political machines of the day and fought vigorously against corruption.

Peter Cooper (1791–1883) of New York City designed and built the "Tom Thumb," the first steam locomotive in the United States. With his money, Cooper founded Cooper Union for the Advancement of Science and Art in New York City's East Village, a tuition-free school for engineers and artists.

Mario Cuomo (1932–) was born in Queens, the son of immigrant parents from Italy. He practiced law and then entered public service. Cuomo served as New York's Secretary of State, Lieutenant Governor, and in 1982 was elected the state's fifty-third governor. As governor, Cuomo championed the rights of women, minorities, and the disabled and worked for social and political reform. Known as a dynamic speaker, he delivered many eloquent speeches during his 12 years in office.

Joseph (Joe) DiMaggio (1914–) was born in California but has been claimed by New York. "The Yankee Clipper" was a New York Yankee's outfielder for 15 years. Voted the American League's most valuable player

in 1939, 1941, and 1947, DiMaggio was elected to the Baseball Hall of Fame in 1955.

George Eastman (1854–1932) was a pioneer in film and photography. Born in Waterville, Eastman was a high-school dropout who became a clerk in a bank in Rochester. Working at night, Eastman devised a way to put film on a roll. In 1880, he founded the Eastman Kodak Company. Eight years later he came out with the first Kodak camera.

Julius Erving (1950–), known as "Dr. J," grew up in Roosevelt, Long Island. Playing basketball for the New York Nets in the 1970s, he invented the "over the rim" technique with his spectacular leaping ability.

George Gershwin (1898–1937) grew up in New York City listening to all kinds of music. As a composer, he blended different musical styles to create with his brother Ira such works as *Rhapsody in Blue,* the musical *Lady Be Good,* and the famous folk opera *Porgy and Bess.*

Mel Gibson (1956–) may have an Australian accent, but he was born in Peekskill. Moving to Australia as a boy, Gibson made his mark in the Australian science fiction films *Mad Max* and *Road Warrior.* He then went to Hollywood, where he became best known for his role as a cop in the *Lethal Weapon* films.

Ruth Bader Ginsburg (1933–), from Brooklyn, graduated first in her class at Harvard. She was the first permanent female law professor at Columbia University and the founder of the Women's Rights Project. Bader Ginsburg also served as a federal judge. In 1993, she became the second woman appointed to the U.S. Supreme Court.

Alexander Hamilton (1755–1804) was born in the West Indies and came to New York City to attend Columbia University. After serving in the American Revolution, Hamilton was appointed secretary of the treasury in the new U.S. government. He laid the foundation for the economic policy of the young United States. Industry, Hamilton believed, would make the nation strong. He fought for the adoption of the U.S. Constitution and founded the New York *Post*, a newspaper that still exists today. He was killed in a duel by Aaron Burr.

Langston Hughes (1902–1967) was born in Joplin, Missouri. Moving to New York City, he became famous as a major poet of the Harlem Renaissance of the 1920s. Much of his work expresses the struggle of African Americans. But Hughes also wrote several children's books, including *The Sweet and Sour Animal Book* and *The Dream Keeper.*

Fiorello La Guardia (1882–1947) was born in New York City. Nicknamed "The Little Flower," he won the hearts of New Yorkers through his honesty and reform programs. As mayor from 1934 to 1945, La Guardia supported urban renewal, the rights of workers, and housing and health programs for the poor. A colorful person, he read the comics to children over the radio during a newspaper strike. Once, as a mediator during a coal strike in the city, he turned off the heat in a meeting room when the two sides could not agree.

Emma Lazarus (1849–1887) was born in New York City. Well-known as a poet, Lazarus also became involved in the cause of Jewish immigrants who were fleeing Russian tyranny in the 1880s. When she was asked to write a verse for the base of the Statue of Liberty, she composed the now-famous poem "The New Colossus."

Barbara McClintock (1902–1992), raised in Brooklyn, spent her career studying genetics. At her laboratory in Cold Spring Harbor, while doing research on corn, she found that genes can "jump" from one chromosome to another. This was a groundbreaking explanation of hereditary patterns. For her discovery, McClintock received the Nobel Prize for Physiology in 1983.

Anna Mary Robertson Moses (1860–1961), known as Grandma Moses, was born in Washington County. For most of her life, she ran her own farm. Moses once said she probably would have raised chickens if she hadn't become a painter. At the age of 80, she began turning out canvases of "old-timey" farm life from her home in Eagle Bridge. Among her 1,000 paintings are *The Old Checkered House, Black Horses,* and *Hoosick Valley (From the Window).*

Joseph Pulitzer (1847–1911), an immigrant from Hungary, became New York City's leading newspaper publisher in the late 1800s. Through his paper, the New York *World,* Pulitzer fought political corruption and crusaded for reform. By 1887, the *World* had the largest circulation of any paper in the nation. Pulitzer went on to found Columbia University's School of Journalism and established the Pulitzer Prizes for achievements in journalism, literature, drama, and music.

Geraldo Rivera (1943–), journalist and TV talk-show host, was born in New York City. As a TV news reporter, he exposed the terrible conditions in a home for the mentally disabled in 1972. Over the years, Rivera has won many awards for his investigative TV reporting and has also worked to help disadvantaged people. Despite his fame, one of his shows did not do well. But Rivera later bounced back as a TV talk-show host with his program *Geraldo.*

Diann Roffe-Steinrotter (1968–) began skiing at the age of two near her home in Rochester. In 1985, she won her first World Cup event—the giant slalom at Lake Placid. She won an Olympic silver medal for the giant slalom in 1992 but kept her sights on winning a gold. In 1994, she triumphed over a bad starting position to win the Women's Super Giant Slalom and her gold medal.

Eleanor Roosevelt (1884–1962) was born in New York City. A humanitarian and reformer, she became known as "The First Lady of the World." She was also the most active of the nation's First Ladies. She wrote her own newspaper column, advised her husband on many issues of the day, and was a strong champion of the rights of African Americans.

Franklin Roosevelt (1882–1945) was born in Hyde Park to a well-to-do and very old New York family. As the thirty-second president, he led the nation during the Great Depression of the 1930s and through World War II. His New Deal programs included social relief and reform and more federal control over business and industry. His radio "Fireside Chats" let Americans know their government was working to help them.

Dr. Jonas Salk (1914–1995), born in New York City, began his research on the polio virus at the University of Pittsburgh, where he developed a vaccine for polio. The first tests on children began in 1952, and by 1955, the vaccine became available for the general public. Before his death, Dr. Salk was working on a vaccine for AIDS.

Beverly Sills (1929–) was born Belle Silverman in New York City. She began performing on the radio at the age of four and went on to become a major opera soprano and recording star. A dynamic and creative manager, she took over the failing New York City Opera in 1980 and greatly improved its finances and its image.

Denzel Washington (1954–), born in Mt. Vernon, first became well-known playing the role of a doctor in the television series *St. Elsewhere*. In 1989,

he won an Oscar as Best Supporting Actor in the film *Glory.* He was also nominated for an Oscar for the film *Cry Freedom,* and he had the lead role in *Malcolm X.*

Edith Wharton (1862–1937), a native of New York City, wrote about the lives and manners of turn-of-the century upper-class New York society. One of her best-known novels, *The Age of Innocence,* won the 1921 Pulitzer Prize for Fiction, and was made into a successful motion picture in 1994.

Vanessa Williams (1963–), raised in Millwood, was the first African-American Miss America. Her musical talent has helped her achieve stardom. Williams's first album, *The Right Stuff,* went gold in 1988, and her second, *Comfort Zone,* went platinum. In 1994, she became the star of the Broadway hit *Kiss of the Spider Woman.*

CALENDAR OF CELEBRATIONS

Saranac Lake celebrates snow and ice in February with the nation's oldest winter carnival. Visitors watch hockey tournaments, skating races, and torchlight skiing. The festival ends with a fireworks display called "storming the ice palace."

New York City's Irish heritage is celebrated in March with the Saint Patrick's Day Parade. For hours, the Grand Marshal leads bagpipers, fife and drum corps, and bands from city departments up Fifth Avenue. Scores of bands from schools and communities around the nation join them. You are likely to see many New York politicians at this parade.

Saranac Lake Festival

Jamestown honors its famous daughter Lucille Ball with an annual Lucyfest. The May celebration includes films as well as live comedy, a good show-case for new comedians. Visitors can tour various "Lucy" sites and go to an auction of Lucy mementos.

Tulips, which came with the early Dutch settlers, are the special feature of Albany's yearly Tulip Festival in May. Some 50,000 blooming tulips compete with music, exhibits, and a bicycle race through the city. A Tulip Queen is crowned at the end of the celebration.

New York City's International Food Festival stretches for 20 blocks along Ninth Avenue. Often called the city's biggest block party, it is also the oldest. Some 300 different foods from about 30 cultures remind New Yorkers of their rich ethnic heritage each May.

A yellow-brick road runs down the center of Chittenango. It honors the town's native son L. Frank Baum, the creator of *The Wizard of Oz*. An annual May Ozfest features an Ozparade and an Ozcraft show.

Old Forge has a unique way to celebrate Father's Day in June. The towns-people hold a frog-jumping contest. From large to small, from fat to thin, frogs leap around on the town's tennis court. There is also an "ugly tie" contest for dads.

Cape Vincent residents celebrate their North Country French Canadian heritage in July with a French Festival. Artisans create traditional crafts, and there is plenty of authentic French food and pastries. Fireworks and a parade top off the festival.

Cobleskill is the home of the yearly Iroquois Indian Festival. On Labor Day weekend, Iroquois men and women gather to celebrate their heritage. They perform special ceremonies and dances, play traditional games, and serve authentic foods. Iroquois crafts are also on display.

A "run for the pasta" is a feature of Watertown's Bravo Italiano Festival in September. Men and women dress in traditional Italian costumes and celebrate their history with food, music, and games. One special game is bocce, an old Italian bowling game.

Paying tribute to the apple is a favorite New York pastime. At Lockport's Apple Country Festival, visitors can view the world's largest cider barrel and feast on apple pancakes in October.

The Harvest Festival at Wappingers Falls in October celebrates the Hudson Valley's early settlers and the valley's environment. Folk songs, banjo bands, and a dance called clogging are featured along with wildlife talks and farm demonstrations.

Visitors and residents begin early to find good spots to view Macy's Thanksgiving Day Parade in New York City. Santa Claus rides by while gigantic balloons depicting famous cartoon characters float overhead.

Macy's Thanksgiving Day Parade

The night before, many people gather to watch as the balloons are inflated near Central Park.

TOUR THE STATE

Fort Ontario (Oswego). Military drills and exhibits trace the history of this fortress, which has been used as a training center and garrison for soldiers from the French and Indian War through World War II.

John Brown State Historic Site (North Elba) is the nineteenth-century farm and burial place of the famous abolitionist.

Lake Placid Winter Olympic Training Center (Lake Placid). In addition to holding all kinds of winter sports events, Lake Placid's Olympic Training Center is a training ground for athletes from around the world.

Ausable Chasm (Ausable). This famous gorge was carved out by the Ausable River on its way to Lake Champlain. Visitors can take an exciting boat ride through the river's swift rapids.

Fort Crailo Museum (Rensselaer) recreates early Dutch life in the Hudson Valley with furniture, household items, and a working kitchen.

National Baseball Hall of Fame Museum (Cooperstown) honors famous baseball players and contains exhibits of historic baseball equipment.

Statue of "Uncle Sam" Wilson, a symbol of the United States

Battle of Saratoga National Historic Park (Stillwater). Signs guide visitors around the sites of the battles on this vast battlefield.

United States Military Academy at West Point conducts parades and reviews for visitors. Its military museum is the largest in the world. You can also see links from a chain that was stretched across the Hudson River to block British ships during the American Revolution.

Sunnyside (Tarrytown) is the home of author Washington Irving. He is most well known for his two tales about early Dutch Settlers, "Rip Van Winkle" and "The Legend of Sleepy Hollow." The home is a unique creation of Irving's. He added gables, fancy chimneys, and a tall tower to the original house.

Franklin D. Roosevelt National Historic Site (Hyde Park) was the home of the thirty-second President. Its library and museum contain many of Roosevelt's books, papers, and personal belongings as well as the papers of Eleanor Roosevelt.

Statue of Liberty National Monument (Liberty Island, New York City). Exhibits at the base of the statue tell the story of immigration from 1600 to the present. Visitors can also walk up into the famous torch held by the Lady with the Lamp.

Ellis Island National Monument (New York City). Restored buildings and exhibits of immigrant artifacts commemorate the thousands of people who passed through the doors of Ellis Island to enter America.

The Brooklyn Children's Museum (New York City). Hands-on exhibits let young visitors jump up and down on giant piano keys to make music or try out beds from different countries. In the Animal Diner, when kids push buttons, animals light up to show the kinds of foods they eat.

The Bronx Zoo (New York City) is the largest city zoo in the country. Nearly 4,000 animals of some 450 different species live in specially arranged open areas that match their natural habitat.

Canondagan "Town of Peace" Historic Site (Victor). Canondagan is the state's only Native American historic site. It is located where a seventeenth-century Seneca village once stood. Signs along trails used by the Seneca tell the story of these people.

Corning Glass Center (Corning) has a factory that makes special art glass. Its library has thousands of books on glassmaking, and a museum contains exhibits covering 3,500 years of glassmaking.

Niagara Falls (Niagara Falls). Visitors can marvel at the power of these waters by taking a boat ride to the foot of the falls or by walking along the base of the falls.

George Eastman House (Rochester) is filled with collections about photography, the technology of film, and camera exhibits. There are nature walks in the gardens. A discovery room encourages hands-on activities.

Women's Rights National Historic Park (Seneca Falls) includes the restored home of Elizabeth Cady Stanton, an early leader in the women's rights movement.

FUN FACTS

Sam Wilson of Troy is said to be the model for our national symbol of the man with the white beard and tall hat. Wilson, called "Uncle Sam" by his friends, sold meat to the army in the War of 1812. He marked the barrels "U.S." When asked what the initials meant, people responded, "Uncle Sam."

New York State got its nickname, "The Empire State," from George Washington. Washington told New York's first governor, George Clinton, that the state would someday become the "seat of Empire."

FIND OUT MORE

If you'd like to find out more about New York, look in your school library, local library, bookstore, or video store for these titles:

BOOKS

America the Beautiful: New York, R. Conrad Stein, Chicago: Childrens Press, 1994.

From Sea to Shining Sea: New York, Dennis Brindell Fradin, Chicago: Childrens Press, 1994.

Hello U.S.A.: New York, Amy Gelman, Minneapolis: Lerner Publications, 1992.

A Historical Album of New York, Monique Avakian and Carter Smith III, Brookfield, CT: Millbrook Press, 1993.

Iroquois Stories: Heroes and Heroines, Monsters and Magic, Joseph Bruchac, Trumansburg, NY: Crossing Press, 1985.

A Kid's Guide to New York City, Peter Lerangis, San Diego: Harcourt Brace Jovanovich, 1988.

Let's Discover the States: Upper Atlantic, New Jersey, New York, Thomas G. and Virginia L. Aylesworth, New York: Chelsea House, 1987.

VIDEOTAPES

I Love New York, Albany: State Library, 1980. 28 minutes. (Describes different areas of New York, as part of Eastman Kodak Company's centennial celebration.)

Pete Seeger's Family Concert, Sony Kids' Music/Sony Wonder, 1992. 45 minutes. (Folksinger Seeger mixes music with a message about New York's environment, in a concert on the banks of the Hudson River.)

COMPUTER DISKS/CD-ROM

New York Jeopardy!: Answers & Questions About Our State, Carole Marsh, Atlanta: Gallopade Publishing Group, 1995. Available in paperback, hardcover, and on computer diskette, Macintosh and Windows versions. (Educational and entertaining answers and questions about New York, based on the popular TV show.)

New York Facts & Factivities!, Carole Marsh, Atlanta: Gallopade Publishing Group, 1996. Mac/Windows CD-ROM. (Computer activities include drawing, writing, matching, and pop quizzes on New York legends, geography, and people.)

INTERNET

On the Internet, go to the State of New York Home Page at www.state.ny.us on the World Wide Web. You will find pictures, information, and suggestions for further research about the state.

INDEX

Page numbers for illustrations are in boldface.